MODERN AMERICAN REMEDIES:
CASES AND MATERIALS

Aspen Publishers

MODERN AMERICAN REMEDIES: CASES AND MATERIALS

Third Edition

2007 Supplement

Douglas Laycock
Yale Kamisar Collegiate Professor of Law
The University of Michigan

Wolters Kluwer

Law & Business

AUSTIN   BOSTON   CHICAGO   NEW YORK   THE NETHERLANDS

Aspen Publishers
Attn: Permissions Department
76 Ninth Avenue, 7th Floor
New York, NY   10011-5201

To contact Customer Care, e-mail customer.care@aspenpublishers.com,
call 1-800-234-1660, fax 1-800-901-9075, or mail correspondence to:

Aspen Publishers
Attn: Order Department
PO Box 990
Frederick, MD 21705

Printed in the United States of America.

1 2 3 4 5 6 7 8 9 0

ISBN 978-0-7355-6961-4

Library of Congress Cataloging-in-Publication Data☐☐☐☐

Laycock, Douglas.☐☐
     Modern American remedies : cases and materials / Douglas☐☐
Laycock. - 3rd ed.☐☐
          ☐p.   cm.☐
     ☐☐Includes index.☐
     ☐☐ISBN 0-7355-2469-6 (casebound)☐
     ☐☐ISBN 0-7355-6430-2 (supplement)☐
     ☐☐1. Remedies (Law) - United States - Cases. I. Title.☐☐
KF9010.A7 L39 2002☐☐   ☐☐☐☐2001056091
347.73'77 - dc21☐☐

About Wolters Kluwer Law & Business

Wolters Kluwer Law & Business is a leading provider of research information and workflow solutions in key specialty areas. The strengths of the individual brands of Aspen Publishers, CCH, Kluwer Law International and Loislaw are aligned within Wolters Kluwer Law & Business to provide comprehensive, in-depth solutions and expert-authored content for the legal, professional and education markets.

CCH was founded in 1913 and has served more than four generations of business professionals and their clients. The CCH products in the Wolters Kluwer Law & Business group are highly regarded electronic and print resources for legal, securities, antitrust and trade regulation, government contracting, banking, pension, payroll, employment and labor, and healthcare reimbursement and compliance professionals.

Aspen Publishers is a leading information provider for attorneys, business professionals and law students. Written by preeminent authorities, Aspen products offer analytical and practical information in a range of specialty practice areas from securities law and intellectual property to mergers and acquisitions and pension/benefits. Aspen's trusted legal education resources provide professors and students with high-quality, up-to-date and effective resources for successful instruction and study in all areas of the law.

Kluwer Law International supplies the global business community with comprehensive English-language international legal information. Legal practitioners, corporate counsel and business executives around the world rely on the Kluwer Law International journals, loose-leafs, books and electronic products for authoritative information in many areas of international legal practice.

Loislaw is a premier provider of digitized legal content to small law firm practitioners of various specializations. Loislaw provides attorneys with the ability to quickly and efficiently find the necessary legal information they need, when and where they need it, by facilitating access to primary law as well as state-specific law, records, forms and treatises.

Wolters Kluwer Law & Business, a unit of Wolters Kluwer, is headquartered in New York and Riverwoods, Illinois. Wolters Kluwer is a leading multinational publisher and information services company.

CONTENTS

PREFACE

This Supplement summarizes the remedies decisions of the United States Supreme Court through the end of the Court's Term on June 29, 2007, the administrative compensation scheme for victims of the terrorist attacks of September 11, 2001, new empirical studies of compensatory and punitive damages in tort cases, and interesting or important developments elsewhere. There are two new principal cases. Philip Morris Co. v. Williams replaces BMW v. Gore and State Farm Mutual Automobile Insurance v. Campbell on constitutional limits on punitive damages, but substantial notes on *BMW* and excerpts from *State Farm* are retained. eBay v. MercExchange is a substantial Supreme Court pronouncement on the standards for issuing permanent injunctions; I have added it between the material on specific performance and undue hardship.

Douglas Laycock
July 1, 2007

CHAPTER TWO

PAYING FOR HARM: COMPENSATORY DAMAGES

A. THE BASIC PRINCIPLE: RESTORING PLAINTIFF TO HIS RIGHTFUL POSITION

Page 15. Before note 1, add:

0.1. Debora Threedy at Utah is writing a history of the background, litigation, and aftermath of *Hatahley*. Among the many things she has learned: The original trial judge unsuccessfully sued the judges of the court of appeals in mandamus to prevent reassignment of the case. Ritter v. Murrah, 362 U.S. 946 (1960). The case eventually settled in the early 1960s for $45,000; $9,000 went to the lawyers for nearly ten years of litigation, and the plaintiffs divided the rest in proportion to the number of animals they had lost. The litigation did not resolve their right to the land, but the government ultimately traded much of the land in dispute to the Navajo in exchange for Navajo land inundated by the Glen Canyon Dam. Professor Threedy believes that the liability judgment in *Hatahley* is the first time that Native Americans prevailed against the federal government on a claim of intentional wrongdoing. The name is pronounced Hah-Tah-Lay, with equal emphasis on all three syllables.

B. VALUE AS THE MEASURE OF THE RIGHTFUL POSITION

Page 24. After note 6, add:

A mistake and a bit of trivia: The mistake is that Learned Hand did not write the opinion. He was on the panel, but his cousin Augustus Hand wrote the opinion. The trivia is that Paul Wangerin at John Marshall, who works on visual images as teaching aides, has discovered a photograph of the *Helen B. Moran*. Although the opinion calls it a barge, it was plainly a self-propelled and self-piloted vessel, as we might have inferred from the fact that it had a name. On the Mississippi, where I grew up, we would have called it a tugboat. A barge was long, flat, and hollow, with no means of propulsion, steering, or braking, designed to be pushed or pulled by a boat the way a locomotive moves train cars or a truck pulls a trailer. The *Helen B. Moran* was none of those things.

Page 25. After note 9, add:

9.1. With damaged automobiles, and sometimes with other kinds of property, repair does not fully restore value. A car that has been wrecked will have a lower resale value, no matter how carefully it is repaired. So can the owner recover repair costs plus the residual loss of value -- the difference between the value before the accident and the value after repair? The D.C. court recently said yes. American Service Center Associates v. Helton, 867 A.2d 235 (D.C. 2005). Similar cases from ten other jurisdictions are collected *id.* at 243 n.11.

This doesn't mean you will collect repair costs plus loss in value from your own insurance company. Insurers have fiercely resisted a recent push for that measure of recovery in collision insurance claims; cases are collected in American Manufacturers Mutual Insurance Co. v. Schaefer, 124 S.W.3d 154 (Tex. 2003). My impression is that the insurers are winning. And in states where they lose, they can rewrite the policy or go to the legislature for relief. They want to pay repair cost, or value before the collision, but no combination of the two.

Page 26. After note 13, add:

14. What if the value of the property taken is zero? See Brown v. Legal Foundation, 538 U.S. 216 (2003), upholding Washington's IOLTA program. The acronym means Interest on Lawyers' Trust Accounts. Lawyers often hold large or small amounts of their clients' money, usually for short periods pending transactions. These funds must be placed in a trust account segregated from the lawyer's own funds. A separate interest-bearing account may be opened for each client, but usually, the amounts are so small or the expected holding time is so short that separate accounts are not practical. Where

separate accounts are not practical, all fifty states now require lawyers to place these funds in a pooled account, the interest from which is used to support legal services for the indigent. These programs raised more than $200 million in 2001.

In Phillips v. Washington Legal Foundation, 524 U.S. 156 (1998), the Court held that the interest on such accounts is the property of individual clients. And in *Brown*, the Court confirmed that the IOLTA program takes this property for public use. But, the Court held, the constitutionally required just compensation is zero, because the value of this interest to the clients, less the administrative cost of calculating it and paying it to them, is zero or less. Four dissenters thought the clients were entitled to the amount of the interest earned, and that there was no basis for subtracting administrative costs.

Page 31. After note 2, add:

Early in the new millennium, the church did substantial restoration work, and its website discussed the foundations. Under the title *Like a Rock: Pilings, Piers, and Foundation*, the church said of the cracks created by the John Hancock construction: "Fortunately, those cracks haven't grown since then. This kind of crack is different than -- and unrelated to -- deterioration of the structural piling system." That page appears to have been taken down; today the website simply says that, "More than 125 years after Trinity's completion, its foundation remains strong." *About the Building*, at
http://www.trinityinspires.org/preservation/who_building_ext.html.

C. RELIANCE AND EXPECTANCY AS MEASURES OF THE RIGHTFUL POSITION

Page 56. After note 4, add:

NOTES ON THE MEASURE OF DAMAGES IN FRAUD CASES

1. There is a vast body of law on damages for fraud, and I do not propose to belatedly review it all here. But I have to tell you a bit more than I have to set the ground for an important new decision.

Smith v. Bolles and similar cases gave rise to the "out-of-pocket" measure of fraud damages, summarized as "the difference between the value of what [plaintiff] has received in the transaction and its purchase price or other value given for it." *Restatement (Second) of Torts* §549(1)(a) (1977). The value of what plaintiff received meant the true value, if all the facts had been known, on the day of the fraudulent transaction. So a plaintiff who buys a stock in January for $15 a share on the basis of a fraudulent misrepresentation, and sells it in December for $10 a share, has not necessarily suffered $5 in damages. The price might have declined for many reasons: the truth came out, the market went down, the company suffered some misfortune unrelated to the fraud. Plaintiff's damages were traditionally said to be the difference between $15 a share and the true value of the stock when purchased in January. Of course there were variations and exceptions, and the price of the stock after the truth came out often had evidentiary value on the stock's true value at the time of the fraud.

The Supreme Court has now unanimously held that simply alleging this traditional measure -- that "the price on the date of purchase was inflated because of the misrepresentation" -- is not enough to state a cause of action for securities fraud. Dura Pharmaceuticals, Inc. v. Broudo, 544 U.S. 336, 340 (2005). The Court said the plaintiff has suffered no loss at that instant, because he could immediately resell the security at the same inflated price. And if he sells later at a loss, that loss might have been caused by the misrepresentation or by any other factor affecting the market price.

Plaintiff must both plead and prove "loss causation" -- that his loss was caused by the misrepresentation.

There is nothing new about taking account of the possibility that a decline in price might be caused by factors unrelated to the fraud. And it is not new to recognize that an investor who buys at a price inflated by fraud, and quickly resells at a price equally inflated by fraud, has an offsetting benefit from the fraud and no net damage. It remains to be seen how *Dura* plays out, but the real change may be to move these issues up front to the pleading stage, and perhaps to include in plaintiff's burden of persuasion an obligation to negate all these alternative explanations.

The Court's analysis also makes more sense in light of the facts of *Dura*. The plaintiff class alleged that Dura overstated its earnings and that it overstated its prospects for government approval of a new asthmatic spray device. When the company announced lower earnings, its shares lost nearly half their value. But the misrepresentation of earnings dropped out of the case because plaintiffs failed to allege that the misrepresentation was knowing. That left government approval of the asthmatic spray device. When the Federal Drug Administration refused to approve the device, Dura's share price "temporarily fell but almost fully recovered within one week." *Id.* at 339. So it is quite plausible that plaintiffs were not damaged -- except for those who joined in the panic selling immediately after the government's decision. The Court might have read this price history as evidence that the stock price was never actually inflated by any misrepresentation about the asthmatic spray device. The Court appears to have read it instead -- or in addition -- as evidence that few class members were damaged even if the price had been inflated.

D. CONSEQUENTIAL DAMAGES

Page 62. After the first paragraph of note 6, add:

The Supreme Court noted the issue in Doe v. Chao, 540 U.S. 614, 626 n.12 (2004). The issue actually presented was whether a plaintiff who proved no actual damages could recover the $1,000 minimum provided by the statute; the Court said no. The court of appeals had rejected plaintiff's claim of emotional distress as uncorroborated and unproven, and his petition for certiorari did not challenge that holding or address the meaning of "actual damages." Justice Ginsburg's dissent for three noted that in the common law torts protecting privacy, emotional distress is generally recoverable. *Id.* at 634 n.4.

E. LIMITS ON THE BASIC PRINCIPLE

1. The Parties' Power to Specify the Remedy

Page 87. After note 10, add:

10.1. The court offered a different reason in Diosdado v. Diosdado, 118 Cal. Rptr. 2d 494 (Cal. Ct. App. 2002). When the husband was caught in adultery in 1993, the couple negotiated a "Marital Settlement Agreement," drafted by his lawyer. It acknowledged a mutual "legal obligation of emotional and sexual fidelity," and provided a remedy for any future episode of infidelity, defined as "any act of kissing on the mouth or touching in any sexual manner." The party in breach of this contract was to be liable for $50,000 in liquidated damages, plus attorneys' fees in the contract case, over and above any property settlement or support obligation in the divorce. The husband got caught again in 1998.

The court held the contract void as against public policy. The no-fault divorce law made fault irrelevant in divorce; it also made the victim's emotional distress irrelevant; this contract was an attempt to make both of those relevant again. The wife had offered to prove that the clause was a reasonable or even conservative estimate of the value of her emotional distress. The divorce law specified an equal division of property, with limited exceptions; this was an attempt to create a new exception.

The court might have said the $50,000 was a penalty as compared to the remedy specified in the divorce law. But the public policy holding reaches further; a contract for actual compensatory damages would have been void on the same grounds.

2. Avoidable Consequences, Offsetting Benefits, and Collateral Sources

Page 108. After note 4, add:

4.1. Perhaps because of the increasing difficulty in funding medical insurance, both medical insurers and even governments are becoming increasingly aggressive about asserting subrogation rights. Aggressive versions of such claims were at issue in three recent Supreme Court cases: Arkansas Department of Health and Human Services v. Ahlborn, 547 U.S. 268 (2006); Sereboff v. Mid Atlantic Medical Services, Inc., 126 S.Ct. 1869 (2006); and Empire Healthchoice Assurance, Inc. v. McVeigh, 126 S.Ct. 2121 (2006). In *Ahlborn*, plaintiff was the agency that administers Arkansas's Medicaid program, the state-federal program that provides medical care to some of the nation's poor; in *Sereboff*, plaintiff was the insurer under an employer-sponsored medical plan; in *Empire Healthchoice*, plaintiff was a Blue Cross company providing medical insurance for federal employees.

In each case, state law or the insurance policy provided that the insurer could recover the entire amount it spent on medical care out of any money the insured recovered from a third party, even if the insured received only a partial recovery. This provision was not directly at issue in *Sereboff* or *Empire Healthchoice*, but it was at the center of the dispute in *Ahlborn*. Ahlborn was a college student who suffered permanent brain damage in an auto accident; the resulting disability and large medical expenses made her eligible for Medicaid. Arkansas stipulated that her personal injury claim was worth more than $3 million, even though she settled for $550,000, apparently because the tortfeasors had inadequate liability insurance. Arkansas had expended about $215,000 on her medical care, and under Arkansas law, the state was entitled to recover the full $215,000 out of her $550,000 recovery. So the state would recover all of its losses, and she would be left with a total net recovery (from the settlement plus the earlier medical payments) of about one-sixth of her losses.

The Supreme Court held that the federal Medicaid law that funded much of Arkansas's program precluded the state's claim.

Ahlborn and the state had to share pro rata; the state recovered about $35,000, the same fraction of its claim that Ahlborn had recovered of hers. The stipulation about the value of her claim makes this allocation seem easy, but of course the state might have vigorously disputed the value of her personal injury claim. Or her settlement agreement with the tortfeasors might have purported to allocate the settlement, allocating high values to lost earnings and pain and suffering and minimizing the recovery allocated to medical expenses. Insurers say they need full recovery of all the benefits they pay to avoid being victimized by such manipulations; advocates for personal injury claimants say they need the full protection of the collateral source rule to avoid overreaching by insurers. However the political battle proceeds, prorating the medical insurer's recovery will sometimes be difficult. And it will not always be required; this was a decision under one highly detailed statute.

Sereboff is more fully discussed in the supplement to 699 and 1117; *Empire Healthchoice* held that the insurer's claim must be decided in state court under state law.

3. The Scope of Liability

Page 116. After note 5, add:

6. The Court relied on *Holmes* to dismiss another RICO claim in Anza v. Ideal Steel Supply Corp., 126 S.Ct. 1991 (2006). Plaintiff and defendant were each other's primary competitors. Plaintiff alleged that defendant had not charged sales tax on cash sales, and had filed false sales tax reports with New York to conceal its tax fraud. This fraud effectively lowered defendant's prices (by saving customers the amount of the tax), and this had allegedly deprived plaintiff of sales. The Court said the allegations, even if true, would not show proximate cause. The state was the direct victim of the fraud, in the Court's view. The Court also said that one reason for proximate cause rules is to avoid difficult and attenuated damage calculations, and it would be difficult to determine just how much of plaintiff's losses were attributable to defendant's failure to pay sales tax.

Justice Thomas vigorously dissented. In *Holmes*, all harm to SIPC and to the customers of the brokerage houses was derived from the harm to the brokerage houses -- because of the fraud, the brokerage houses could not meet their obligations, and those to whom they owed obligations were harmed. Many cases fit this pattern -- A injures B, who is then unable to perform obligations to C, but C does not thereby get a claim against A. But here, the harm to New York was no part of the causal chain that harmed plaintiff. New York had not defaulted on any obligation to plaintiff, and defendant had not collected sales tax and failed to pay it over. Plaintiff's claim was that defendant had stolen his customers by offering them an illegal deal that spared them paying sales tax. Elaborating Justice Thomas's point just a little, the only way defendant could profit by this scheme was by attracting additional business; plaintiff was in fact the direct target of the fraud.

Justice Breyer also concurred separately on this issue. He thought the proximate cause of plaintiff's harm was a price cut, not the tax fraud. And price cuts are not illegal; price competition is at the heart of antitrust policy. The illegal way in which defendant funded the price cut was "beside the point as long as the price cut itself is legitimate."

7. The *Holmes* problem arises frequently in construction litigation, where a job site typically has a general contractor and many subcontractors, and sometimes layers of sub and sub-subcontractors. Some of these disputes are simplified with what is called "pass-through litigation." In the most common case, the general contractor is permitted to sue the owner on behalf of himself and his subs. The general must at least conditionally concede that he has liability to the subs, and pass through any recovery obtained on their behalf. The cases are collected in Interstate Contracting Corp. v. City of Dallas, 135 S.W.3d 605 (Tex. 2004). Pass-through litigation is standard practice in federal contract litigation against the United States, and the Texas court reports that nineteen states have adopted the procedure; only Connecticut has rejected it.

Page 119. After note 9, add:

The Florida Supreme Court reversed in both cases. Gracey v. Eaker, 837 So.2d 348 (Fla. 2002); Rowell v. Holt, 850 So.2d 474 (Fla. 2003). Each opinion reaffirmed the impact rule and confined its holding to its facts. *Gracey* relied on statutory protection for psychotherapeutic confidences and on cases holding that impact is not needed when emotional distress is the principal harm to be expected from a tort. *Rowell* relied on the egregiousness of the malpractice and the clarity of causation, and suggested that the holding would not apply to all claims of legal malpractice. The opinion also reveals that the decisive lost document was a restoration of plaintiff's civil rights, entitling him to carry a firearm despite a felony conviction in the sixties.

Reading these opinions clarified a doctrinal relationship that should have been clear from the beginning. The economic harm rule -- no recovery for economic harm without physical impact -- is parallel to the rule in most jurisdictions that negligently inflicted emotional distress is generally not recoverable without some additional threshold showing, of which the most common is accompanying physical injury. See main volume at 191-193. These two cases probably fit more comfortably there than here. But Florida's vocabulary -- the impact rule -- focuses attention on the common theme: with some important exceptions, there is no recovery in negligence for non-physical harm without physical impact.

5. Substantive Policy Goals

Page 144. After note 3, add:

3.1. *Hoffman* set off a further round of litigation about its reach. Employers and others responsible for workplace injuries began to argue that an illegal alien injured on the job could not recover lost wages, or could recover only at the wage rates prevailing in his home country. Many of these cases are collected in Balbuena v. IDR Realty LLC, 845 N.E.2d 1246 (N.Y. 2006). *Balbuena* holds the injured employee entitled to recover lost wages; the dissenters would have said he was trying to recover the benefit of an illegal bargain, and that even if New York permitted such a recovery, it would be preempted by federal immigration law. Some of the cases are collected *id.* at 1256 n.5. My impression is that defendants are losing most of these cases, but I have not done anything like a count of cases.

Page 145. After note 6, add:

6.1. The latest in a line of decisions limiting application of the exclusionary rule is Hudson v. Michigan, 126 S.Ct. 2159 (2006), refusing to exclude evidence found after a violation of the rule that police must generally knock and announce their presence before breaking down the door to conduct a search. The opinion holds no more than that. But its discussion of how civil suits for damages and internal police discipline are effective deterrents of police misconduct seems to invite a more general attack on the exclusionary rule. The problem is that this discussion is wholly illusory. There are few civil suits, because criminal defendants make unsympathetic plaintiffs, and without the exclusionary rule, there is no incentive for internal police discipline.

F. DAMAGES WHERE VALUE CANNOT BE MEASURED IN DOLLARS

1. Personal Injuries and Death

Page 153. After note 8, add:

9. Experimenters asked law students and lay people to award damages for a series of significant but not catastrophic personal injuries. Some respondents were simply told to award "appropriate" compensation; this is roughly equivalent to the standard jury instruction in most states. Some were told to award the amount that would be required to make them whole if they had suffered these injuries. And some were told to award the amount they would demand to suffer these injuries in a voluntary transaction. The results are not very clearly explained, but the basic pattern is

unmistakable. After controlling for outliers, the make-whole instruction roughly doubled the awards, and the selling-price instruction roughly doubled them again. Edward J. McCaffery, Daniel J. Kahneman, and Matthew L. Spitzer, *Framing the Jury: Cognitive Perspectives on Pain and Suffering Awards*, 81 Va. L. Rev. 1341 (1995).

The team also got an interesting set of responses to a survey of lawyers and judges. All recognized that the Golden Rule argument was prohibited in their jurisdiction, and most thought the selling-price argument prohibited, absurd, or both, but a large minority said they had seen plaintiffs' lawyers subtly slip elements of these approaches into their jury argument, and some offered ways to do it without creating reversible error.

Page 153. After note 1, add:

1.1. The Fifth Circuit upheld the trial court's discretion to admit the testimony of a "grief expert" in Vogler v. Blackmore, 352 F.3d 150, 153, 155-156 (5th Cir. 2003). The opinion notes that other courts have upheld the trial court's discretion to exclude such testimony. The opinion does not summarize the grief expert's testimony; it does note that she also described herself as a thanatologist.

Page 161. After note 10, add:

10.1. In some states, wrongful death damages are awarded as a lump sum to all persons entitled to recover, and then apportioned among the individual plaintiffs in a supplemental proceeding. See, e.g., Cal. Civ. Proc. Code §377.61 (2004). The California court has agreed to decide questions about the relevance of character evidence in such an apportionment proceeding. Corder v. Corder, 34 Cal. Rptr. 3d 294 (Cal. App.), *review granted*, 125 P.3d 290 (Cal. 2005). The case is still undecided as of June 30, 2007.

Both the facts and the opinions in the court of appeals are flamboyant. The widow and an adult daughter by a previous marriage jointly settled with defendant for a lump sum of $1.1 million. The widow and decedent had been married for eight months. The daughter presented several witnesses who testified that decedent had intended to divorce his wife. "According to them the decedent felt that his marriage was a mistake because his wife had continued to work as a prostitute despite her promises to stop." 34 Cal. Rptr. 3d at 298. The trial court found this testimony to be true. The court also found that decedent had a close relationship with his adult daughter, and that he had repeatedly bailed her out financially, although the dissenter said she was not financially dependent. Finding that the marriage would soon have ended, the trial court awarded 90% of the settlement to the adult daughter, and the court of appeals affirmed.

The dissenter was outraged. California takes a relative narrow view of what counts as pecuniary damages, and does not permit recovery for any form of emotional loss. The wife, and only the wife, had a legal claim to financial support. The adult daughter had no claim to financial support. Defendant would never have agreed to pay anything like $1.1 million to the adult daughter; the principal source of the settlement was the wife's claim. The charges of misbehavior by the widow were easy to manufacture, totally uncorroborated by anything but hearsay about what the decedent had allegedly said, and in effect a proceeding for divorce based on fault -- a generation after California enacted no-fault divorce as the exclusive means of ending marriages.

Page 162. After note 12, add:

NOTES ON REMEDIES FOR SEPTEMBER 11 VICTIMS

1. The terrorist attacks of September 11, 2001 inflicted nearly 3,000 wrongful deaths and a comparable number of nonfatal injuries. Congress responded with an extraordinary set of remedies that gave the public a look at the difficulty of measuring wrongful death damages. Title IV of the Air Transportation Safety and System Stabilization Act, rushed to passage on September 22, and strangely codified as a note to 49 U.S.C. §40101, created a federal cause of action for "damages arising out of the hijacking and subsequent crashes" of the four flights. It provided that this cause of action would be the exclusive judicial remedy, that the Southern District of

New York would have exclusive jurisdiction of all claims, and that the governing substantive law would be "derived from the law" of the state in which each crash occurred, "unless such law is inconsistent with or preempted by Federal law." And it limited the liability of each airline to the amount of its liability insurance.

2. Alternatively, the Act created an administrative remedy funded by the federal government. Suing any defendant in court waived the right to the administrative remedy; filing an administrative claim waived the right to sue in court. The regulations provided that victims could sue knowing participants in the terrorist conspiracy without waiving their right to the administrative remedy. Many claimants waited until near the deadline late in 2003, but in the end, 98% of the families of deceased victims, and 4,400 surviving personal injury victims, filed administrative claims. Some 60 families elected to sue the airlines and other defendants in federal court. Anthony DePalma, *Airlines Want 9/11 Lawsuits From Families Thrown Out*, N.Y. Times A32 (May 2, 2003), available at 2003 WLNR 5190129. Seven families, too depressed or grief stricken to take any action, failed to file either a lawsuit or an administrative claim, despite repeated personal appeals from senior officials responsible for the administrative remedy.

3. To implement the administrative remedy, the Attorney General was directed to appoint a Special Master to determine no-fault compensation for "economic and noneconomic losses" of all victims who filed a claim, and to subtract from this amount "all collateral sources, including life insurance, pension funds, death benefit programs, and payments by Federal, State, or local governments related to the terrorist-related aircraft crashes of September 11, 2001." Awards to victims who were injured but survived were to be determined on an individual basis in an administrative proceeding. The Special Master published compensation schedules for death claims. All the work of the Special Master, including his rules for calculating benefits, are set out in Final Report of the Special Master for the September 11th Victim Compensation Fund of 2001, available at *www.usdoj.gov/final_report.pdf* and *www.usdoj.gov/final_report_vol2.pdf.*

4. The Special Master awarded $250,000 for the "noneconomic loss" of each decedent, plus $100,000 for the "noneconomic loss" of each spouse and each dependent of a decedent. Recognizing that "each person experienced the unspeakable events of that day in a unique way," he found these circumstances generally unknowable for decedents. He defended the $250,000 figure as "roughly equivalent to the amounts received under existing federal programs" for public safety officers and military personnel killed in the line of duty. Some victims and their representatives criticized it as far less than a jury would award.

5. Some victims were bitterly critical of the offset of collateral sources; lawyers suggested that some victims might recover nothing from the fund. The Special Master responded to that criticism by deciding that contributions from private donors, 401(k) plans, and the large special tax exemptions enacted for victims would not be treated as collateral sources. He also announced his "expectation" that when the individual needs of each family were considered, "it will be very rare that a claimant will receive less than $250,000." This expectation appears to have required some creative statutory interpretation, but in fact, no claimant received less than $250,000 for the loss of a deceased victim.

6. The Special Master processed 2,968 death claims and paid 2,880 of them; 88 were denied, withdrawn, or abandoned. He processed 4,435 personal injury claims and paid 2,680; 1,755 were denied, withdrawn, or abandoned. The Special Master completed his work in 2004; all the money -- more than $7 billion -- was distributed within three years of the attacks.

7. Wrongful death awards ranged from the $250,000 minimum to $7.1 million -- and this with no jury and a fixed amount for "noneconomic" loss. The variation resulted from income, age, dependents, and the subtraction of collateral sources. Because the affluent were more likely to be well insured, income did not make as much difference as might have been expected. There were minimum awards even at the highest income levels, including six for decedents who had earned more than $220,000 a year. The awards did generally increase with income, but the curve was pretty flat in the middle income ranges. Awards were calculated to the penny, but I am rounding off:

Income Range	Largest Award
$0-20 thousand	$2.5 million
$20-40 thousand	$3.0 million
$40-60 thousand	$4.1 million
$60-80 thousand	$4.3 million
$80-100 thousand	$4.4 million
$100-120 thousand	$4.5 million
$120-140 thousand	$5.0 million
$140-160 thousand	$4.2 million
$160-180 thousand	$5.4 million
$180-200 thousand	$5.5 million
$200-220 thousand	$5.3 million
over $220 thousand	$7.1 million

The mean award was $2.1 million; the median was $1.7 million.

8. The Special Master denied putting any cap on awards, but he also plainly indicated reluctance to give full weight to extremely high incomes. He argued that such incomes might not continue for a lifetime, and that in any event, the families did not need the huge awards that would be produced by projecting such incomes over a lifetime. Families of high-income employees from Cantor Fitzgerald, the investment banking firm that lost so many employees near the top of One World Trade Center, alleged that the Special Master was applying a de facto cap. The lead plaintiff claimed to have economic losses between $28 and $52 million; the Special Master's consultant, Price Waterhouse, calculated these losses at $14 to $15 million.

By various routes, the court allowed the Special Master to do it his way. Schneider v. Feinberg, 345 F.3d 135 (2d Cir. 2003). It rejected likely tort awards as not comparable, because tort litigation requires aggressive litigation and long delays, attorneys' fees must be subtracted, and defendants might go bankrupt. The Special Master's award would be "simple, certain, non-contentious, and prompt." Id. at 144. It agreed that the duration of very high earnings was unpredictable. The court plainly had some residual skepticism about the Special Master's professed unwillingness to award very large sums, but the statute protected his awards from judicial review after they were made, and in effect, the court held them equally unreviewable before they were made. "So while we agree with plaintiffs that the Special Master's comments are hard to square with the text of the Act, we decline to declare what we cannot enforce." *Id.* at 145.

9. The Special Master's files would seem to hold a treasure trove of data for some empirically minded scholar. The results of his process confirm that the large variations in wrongful death awards do not result merely from the vagaries of juries, and that choices about the collateral source rule may have different average consequences at different income levels. The process itself suggests that it is possible to calculate damages with a sophisticated schedule, to process large numbers of claims quickly and efficiently, and to distribute substantial sums in compensation. But nothing about the process suggests that it is politically possible to implement more generally any lessons we might learn from it.

10. The Special Master published a complex formula for determining economic loss in wrongful death cases, based principally on earnings history, age, and number of dependents, and generally tracking a sophisticated understanding of existing law on lost earnings. That formula is reviewed in this supplement to page 228.

Less information has been published about personal injury awards, which ranged from $500 to $8.6 million, averaging about $1.85 million. A majority of the personal injury awards were for respiratory distress from breathing fumes around the destroyed buildings. A Reuters story on June 4, 2004, reported that the $8.6 million went to a woman who was hit by falling debris from the second plane. The falling metal split open her back, punctured her intestines, sliced off her buttocks, and crushed her legs; she was hospitalized for a year and faces additional reconstructive surgery.

For a symposium with articles by some of the nation's leading torts scholars, see *After Disaster: The September 11th Compensation Fund and the Future of Civil Justice*, 53 DePaul L. Rev. 205 (2003). For the Special Master's own account, see volume 1 of his Final Report, or for a more lively and personal version, Kenneth Feinberg, *What Is Life Worth? The Unprecedented Effort to Compensate the Victims of 9/11* (PublicAffairs 2005).

Page 173. After note 5, add:

5.1. The Justice Department repeated the study in 2001. *Bureau of Justice Statistics Bulletin, Civil Trial Cases and Verdicts in Large Counties, 2001* (NCJ 202803, April 2004). The basic patterns persisted. Perhaps the most surprising finding is that the *median* verdict in cases tried to juries and won by plaintiffs declined substantially, from $65,000 in 1992 to $37,000 in 2001. The number of jury trials has declined, so it is not that more small cases are going to trial. These data are consistent with anecdotal evidence that jurors are responding to the publicity from defense-side efforts to change the law. This response appears to be concentrated in smaller cases with less egregious injuries; the *mean* jury award in tort cases won by plaintiffs increased slightly faster than inflation, from $430,000 in 1996 to $565,000 in 2001. Means are still not reported, but the data for calculating them is available in Table 6.

Other studies are reviewed in Neil Vidmar, *Experimental Simulations and Tort Reform: Avoidance, Error, and Overreaching in Sunstein et al.'s Punitive Damages*, 53 Emory L.J. 1359, 1366-1371 (2004). The empirical studies are growing in weight and consistency. There are extreme outlier verdicts, most of which are reduced by judges or by settlements pending appeal. I have presented representative data with little comment through three editions, and both sides do play games with the data, but it seems increasingly clear that apart from these outlier verdicts, there is remarkably little evidence of a tort crisis. By now, the defense-side advocates could take credit for taming any tort crisis that might have existed -- except that they seem to think the crisis continues unabated and that we need still more restrictions on tort remedies.

One category of outliers is reviewed in W. Kip Viscusi, *The Blockbuster Punitive Damage Awards*, 53 Emory L.J. 1405 (2004). He found 64 punitive damage awards in excess of $100 million. Of these 64 verdicts, 27 came from only two states (Texas and California), and 34 came from 1999 to 2003. These concentrations plainly suggest a change in jury behavior rather than a change in tortfeasing. But judgment had been entered and affirmed on only one of these verdicts. Fifteen had been reversed, nine had been reduced, 27 had been settled, eight appeals were still pending. Professor

Viscusi had no information on two cases. He reported two as "no change," perhaps implying that litigation had been abandoned: one of these defendants was out of business and judgment proof and the other, a murderer, had been extradited and was presumably imprisoned.

Page 173. After note 6, add:

6.1. History repeats itself with variations. Early in the new millennium, peaking in 2002, a new crisis emerged in medical malpractice insurance, especially for obstetricians. Insurers were withdrawing from the market, and doctors were refusing to deliver babies. Explanations from both sides are summarized in an in-depth Wall Street Journal story with multiple headlines: Rachel Zimmerman & Christopher Oster, *Assigning Liability - Insurers' Missteps Helped Provoke Malpractice "Crisis," - Lawsuits Alone Didn't Cause Premiums to Skyrocket; Earlier Price War a Factor - Delivering Ms. Kline's Baby*, Wall St. J. A1 (June 24, 2002).

Insurance industry sources confirm the basic outlines of the story. In the wake of the mid-80s insurance crisis, the St. Paul Companies emerged as the leading medical malpractice carrier. In addition, associations of doctors formed a number of small mutual companies. St. Paul continued to aggressively raise premiums, but actually achieved some savings in the wake of tort reform. Its reserves grew to levels greater than anticipated losses, and from 1992 to 1997, it "released" $1.1 billion in excess reserves; the accounting effect was to report this amount as income. Seeing these reports from St. Paul, the small mutual companies decided that medical malpractice insurance had become a highly profitable business. Did you ever hear about that in the tort reform debate?

The mutuals expanded aggressively and underpriced St. Paul; the result was the price war referenced in the headline. The raging bull market of the late 90s played the role of the high interest rates in the early 80s; investment profits sustained profitability even at low premiums. An industry trade association says that in 2000, insurers collectively paid out $1.36 in claims and expenses for every $1.00 in premiums. This could not go on, and the collapse of the bubble in internet and dot com stocks hastened the end. St. Paul reported a

$980 million loss on medical malpractice insurance in 2001 (just about erasing the earlier $1.1 billion profit), and it withdrew from the business. Other insurers began withdrawing from whole states, and doubling or even quadrupling premiums in states where they remained. Doctors could not pass on the rising costs, because the medical insurers and managed care companies would not permit it.

The industry concedes that this insurance-cycle story aggravated the problem, but it insists that the major problem is a new increase in verdicts. There are the usual dueling and largely unexplained statistics. I summarize some of that data here, more to show the games people play than because these data actually help resolve anything. The industry association says the total cost of claims went up 52% in 5 years, from 1995 to 2000 -- considerably more than inflation but just under 9% a year compounded, and nowhere near the doubling or quadrupling that occurred in premiums. A consumer advocate cites data from A.M. Best, a well-known company that rates the financial strength of insurers, projecting an increase of 47%, apparently over 10 years, but the time frame is not clear. Jury Verdict Research says that the median malpractice verdict in its data base went up 175% from 1994 to 2000, with the 2000 median at $1 million; and that the median verdict for malpractice in childbirth increased to $2,050,000. It also concedes that it collects its cases unsystematically, and that it knows nothing about the cases it is missing except that it does not report on settlements or the 62% of cases won by defendants. There is a clear indicator here that their data is skewed toward the biggest cases: their increase in median is much greater than the industry's reported increase in mean, but if the data covered the same set of cases, it should be the other way around. The reported A.M. Best data is that the average total cost of a claim, including legal expenses and benefits paid, and averaging in the cases won by defendants, will be $42,473 for claims arising in 2000.

6.2. For a much more sophisticated scholarly explanation of the insurance cycle, see Tom Baker, *Medical Malpractice and the Insurance Underwriting Cycle*, 54 DePaul L. Rev. 393 (2005). Changes in claims do not explain the history of sudden and sharp changes in premiums and availability. Changes in interest rates explain some of it. The rest of the explanation depends on factors internal to the insurance industry, including uncertainty, capacity constraints, greed in good times, and fear in bad times. The effect of such factors is amplified in insurance lines with long tails -- that is, long time lags between collecting the premiums and paying the last of the claims. The insurance cycle can be especially violent in medical malpractice because medical malpractice claims have an especially long tail.

6.3. Scholars have finally gotten access to some insurance industry claims data. Several states began systematically collecting such data after earlier insurance crises; two states, Texas and Florida, make that data publicly available, and scholars have finally discovered it. (It is a safe bet that in the other states, the industry successfully lobbied to keep the data secret.) The Texas data on medical malpractice claims are reviewed in Bernard Black, Charles Silver, David A. Hyman, & William M. Sage, *Stability, Not Crisis: Medical Malpractice Claim Outcomes in Texas, 1988-2002*, 2 J. Empirical Legal Stud. 207 (2005).

In Texas, the number of malpractice claims grew at about the rate of population growth, and grew more slowly than health care spending or the number of physicians. The number of small claims declined sharply; the authors infer that they are being driven out of the system by litigation costs and the tort reform movement. Payouts per large claim paid rose very slightly, about 1/10 to 1/2 percent a year in real dollars. If the authors had not taken account of the decline in the number of small claims, they would have found that the mean payout increased by 40%. If they had also failed to adjust for inflation, they would have found that the mean payout increased by 112%! And no doubt your legislators are regularly given such unadjusted data.

Similar data from Florida are reviewed in Neil Vidmar, Paul Lee, Kara MacKillop, Kieran McCarthy, & Gerald McGwin, *Uncovering the "Invisible" Profile of Medical Malpractice Litigation: Insights from Florida*, 54 DePaul L. Rev. 315 (2005). This study found similar stability in the number of claims, and a similar squeezing out of small claims, but real growth in mean and median awards. The Florida team recognized that the reduction in small claims contributed to the growth in mean and median awards, but did not attempt (or did not have sufficient data) to control for that effect.

6.4. The DePaul Law Review has published a massive and highly informative symposium on damages for pain and suffering. *Symposium: Who Feels Their Pain? The Challenge of Noneconomic Damages in Civil Litigation*, 55 DePaul L. Rev. 249 (2006). An introductory essay summarizes the thesis of each article, so you can find the points of greatest interest.

Page 174. After note 8, add:

8.1. The Wisconsin court relied on this theory to strike down a cap of $350,000, adjusted for inflation, on "noneconomic" damages in medical malpractice cases without a claim of wrongful death. Ferdon v. Wisconsin Patients Compensation Fund, 701 N.W.2d 440 (Wis. 2005). "[T]he burden of the cap falls entirely on the most seriously injured victims of medical malpractice." *Id.* at 465. Plaintiffs with small injuries get fully compensated; plaintiffs with more serious injuries do not. "[W]hen the legislature shifts the economic burden of medical malpractice from insurance companies and negligent health care providers to a small group of vulnerable, injured patients, the legislative action does not appear rational." *Id.* at 466 The classification is not "germane to any objective of the law." *Id.*

The court also cited a number of statistical studies to conclude that there is no rational relationship between damage caps and the legislature's goals -- not even the goal of lower premiums for the state's excess liability fund. The dissenters argued that this part of the opinion ignored both common sense and other statistical studies, and that in any event, it intruded much further into legislative fact finding than could be justified under the rational basis test. The majority said that its holding would not lead to invalidation of all caps, although the holding about discrimination against the most seriously injured would seem to apply to all caps.

Numerous decisions from other states, mostly upholding damage caps, are collected *id.* at 448 n.12; *id.* at 513-14 & n.83 (Prosser, J., dissenting).

Page 177. After note 5, add:

5.1. Thinking about such questions has led to a proliferation of categories and labels that inevitably overlap. The Texas court collects cases struggling with the distinctions among pain and suffering, physical impairment, and loss of capacity to enjoy life, in Golden Eagle Archery, Inc. v. Jackson, 116 S.W.3d 757 (Tex. 2003). In many states, these difficulties present questions of how to craft jury instructions; in Texas, where juries are often asked to separately value distinct items of damage, they present more difficult questions of how to review the sufficiency of small awards for some items, and the alleged excessiveness of large awards for other items, where the items may overlap. The *Golden Eagle* jury awarded separate sums for medical care, physical pain and mental anguish, loss of vision, other physical impairment, disfigurement, and loss of earnings in the past. It awarded zero for physical impairment other than loss of vision. None of these terms were defined in a jury instruction, and the facts plaintiff emphasized under other physical impairment went to temporary loss of capacity to enjoy life during his hospitalization. The court upheld the verdict, noting that the jury might reasonably have treated these damages under pain and suffering instead of physical impairment.

Page 179. After note 7, add:

7.1. What if it turned out that plaintiffs' lawyers didn't bother doing the work required to prove up these kinds of future expenses, because pain and suffering got the same dollars with much less work? Then the sensible response to caps on pain-and-suffering damages would be to do the work to prove up these future medical and rehabilitation expenses. That is the intuition that explains an otherwise remarkable empirical finding: after "controlling for the independent effects of severity of injury, as well as numerous additional litigant characteristics, state law, and county demographic variables, noneconomic damages caps have no statistically significant effect on the size of overall compensatory damages, as reflected in either jury verdicts or final judgments." Catherine M.

Sharkey, *Unintended Consequences of Medical Malpractice Damages Caps*, 80 N.Y.U. L. Rev. 391, 469 (2005).

Professor Sharkey also found, not surprisingly, that "severity of injury has a positive and statistically significant effect upon plaintiffs;' recovery of compensatory damages." *Id.* Her data set was the 557 medical malpractice cases in which plaintiff recovered from a physician or corporate health provider, drawn from a larger sample of state-court tort litigation in 1992, 1996, and 2001 in 46 of the nation's 75 most populous counties, originally collected by the National Center for State Courts. The article is also a highly valuable survey of enacted tort reform legislation and empirical studies of the effects of such legislation.

Page 180. After note 9, add:

Other studies using the same, or at least a very similar, nine-level scale have found similar results. The Florida study led by Neil Vidmar, described in more detail at supplement to page 173, applied the scale to Florida medical malpractice claims. These data included settlements. Injuries that were emotional only led to smaller payouts than temporary and slight physical injuries. Death led to smaller payouts than significant, major, or grave permanent injuries. Within the nonfatal physical injuries in levels two through eight, payouts increased steadily with each level. Neil Vidmar, Paul Lee, Kara MacKillop, Kieran McCarthy, & Gerald McGwin, *Uncovering the "Invisible" Profile of Medical Malpractice Litigation: Insights from Florida*, 54 DePaul L. Rev. 315, 340 tbl. 7 (2005).

Page 181. After note 10, add:

10.1. The Fifth Circuit experience with comparative review of verdicts is reviewed, and found very bad, in Lawrence James Madigan, *Excessive Damage Review in the Fifth Circuit: A Quagmire of Inconsistency*, 34 Tex. Tech L. Rev. 429 (2003). Some panels don't do it; the panels that do have evolved a mechanical jurisprudence in which the awards are limited to 50% (or 33%, or 0%, depending on the panel) more than the highest reported award for the same injury in the circuit (in federal question cases) or the state (for diversity cases). Giving controlling weight to a single verdict puts pressure on the choice of analogous verdicts, and some of the choices have been dubious. Despite a strong rule in the Fifth Circuit of treating panel opinions as binding on all other panels, panels apparently feel free to use or ignore this procedure. For an example of the procedure in action, see Vogler v. Blackmore, 352 F.3d 150, 156-160 (5th Cir. 2003).

2. Dignitary and Constitutional Harms

Page 187. After note 1, add:

New York settled the *Tyson* class action with a compensation formula that might lead to payments of as much as $50 million to the class. Stephanie Flanders, *Manhattan: Strip-Search Settlement*, N.Y. Times B3 (June 14, 2001), available at 2001 WLNR 3355486. Boston and Suffolk County settled a similar class action for $10 million. Katherine Zezima, *Massachusetts: Strip-Search Settlement*, N.Y. Times A3 (June 1, 2002), available at 2002 WLNR 4082482. Another class action has been filed based on similar strip searches in Brooklyn. Daniel Wise, *City Loses in Bid to Disqualify Former Counsel*, N.Y.L.J. 1 (June 3, 2002).

Page 193. After note 6, add:

7. There is a good debate on these issues in Norfolk & Western Ry. v. Ayers, 538 U.S. 135 (2003), another railroad case under the Federal Employers Liability Act. The majority holds that plaintiffs with asbestosis have suffered physical injury and can therefore sue for associated emotional distress, including the fear of later contracting cancer, provided that plaintiff must "prove that his alleged fear is genuine and serious." *Id.* at 157. Asbestosis patients have a higher risk of cancer, but even so, only about ten percent eventually get cancer.

Four dissenters thought that asbestosis supported only a claim for emotional distress from asbestosis, not distress based on fear of cancer that would probably never be contracted. They thought the requirement of genuine and serious fear illusory, and that the decision opened the floodgates to a new category of asbestos claims that would bankrupt more asbestos defendants. The minority of plaintiffs who eventually got cancer would be less likely to receive any compensation, because all the money would have been paid out in claims for fear of cancer.

Page 200. After note 3, add:

Compare Rowell v. Holt, 850 So.2d 474 (Fla. 2003), more fully described in main volume and supplement at 118-119, where a jury awarded $16,500 for the emotional distress of a clearly innocent man jailed for 13 days.

G. TAXES, TIME, AND THE VALUE OF MONEY

Page 213. After note 1, add:

The sentence in parentheses in note 1 turns out to be wrong. Mea culpa. Compounding at the municipal bond rate *could* make taxes and the timing of taxes irrelevant -- but only if the interest awarded would not be taxed. Here the interest awarded would be fully taxable, because interest on the judgment would not be interest on a municipal bond. It would plainly be undercompensatory to award interest at the municipal bond rate when we know that plaintiff will have to pay tax on that interest.

Page 214. After note 5, add:

5.1. Kansas v. Colorado has returned to the Court, 543 U.S. 86 (2004), and the ultimate result may be unique. In 1949, the two states divided the waters of the Arkansas River in an interstate compact. Colorado negligently violated the pact from the beginning, and knew or should have known it was violating beginning in 1968. Kansas filed suit in 1985, and the first judgment was entered in 1994. Relying partly on the recommendations of the Special Master (appointed to find facts and make recommendations in this case within the Supreme Court's original jurisdiction) and partly on its own discretion, the Court adjusted all damages for inflation, but awarded interest only on damages accruing after 1985. Interest is often thought of as compensating for inflation plus a real rate of return on investment, so this odd compromise could easily be thought of as partial interest. Omitting the real rate of return on all the years from 1950 to 1985 mattered; it reduced the total judgment from $53 million to something under $38 million.

Page 215. After note 8, add:

8.1. Many courts award prejudgment interest at the prime rate, as in *National Gypsum* on remand. The Ninth Circuit generally awards the rate on 52-week Treasury bills as prejudgment interest, relying on the postjudgment interest statute by analogy. But a different line of Ninth Circuit cases awards a higher rate in takings cases. The Constitution requires just compensation, and some courts have read that to require a fully compensatory interest rate. The Ninth Circuit defines that rate as the rate that could be earned by a reasonably prudent investor investing in a "wide range of government and private obligations with both short term and long term maturities." Both lines of cases are collected in Schneider v. County of San Diego, 285 F.3d 784, 791-794 (9th Cir. 2002).

Page 228. After Problem 2-1, add:

MORE NOTES ON REMEDIES FOR SEPTEMBER 11 VICTIMS

1. The administrative formula for calculating presumptive economic losses of persons killed in the terrorist attacks of September 11 is summarized in volume I of the Final Report of the Special Master for the September 11th Victim Compensation Fund of 2001, available at *www.usdoj.gov/final_report.pdf*; the regulations are reprinted in volume II, available at *www.usdoj.gov/final_report_vol2.pdf*. This formula illustrates many factors that are legally relevant in most jurisdictions, but that are not illustrated in *Jones & Laughlin*. These calculation methods were upheld against a broad range of legal attacks in Schneider v. Feinberg, 345 F.3d 135 (2d Cir. 2003).

2. The Special Master's calculation started with age and the last three years of after-tax income, plus fringe benefits. The formula ignored income above the 98th percentile, or about $231,000. The Special Master heard individualized evidence in cases of higher income, but apparently did not give full weight to that income.

3. Working-life expectancy was based on actuarial data from a study done in 1997-98; it assumed that an employed 25-year-old will work another 33.6 years, and that this number declines gradually to 4.2 years for an employed 65-year-old. Actual working-life expectancy for women is somewhat lower than for men, but the male data was used for both sexes.

4. Annual increases in income were projected forward assuming 2% inflation, 1% productivity gain, and an additional component for "life-cycle or age-specific increase." This last component varied with age, so that the projected earnings growth rate for an 18-year old was 9.7% annually, declining gradually to 3% for workers 52 and over. That is, workers 52 and over were presumed to have exhausted their life-cycle gains, and to experience only general inflation and productivity gains. This is roughly consistent with *Jones & Laughlin*, because decedent there was 52 or close to it, and inflation and general productivity gains would have been the principal source of his salary increases. But for a younger worker, the life-cycle component adds far more than inflation and general productivity. The life-cycle component tends to be greater in more skilled occupations, and in an individual trial, evidence of this factor can be offered on an individual basis.

5. All projected earnings were reduced by 3% to allow for the risk of unemployment.

6. The victim's share of household consumption was subtracted, using average data by income and family size derived from the Consumer Expenditure Survey of the Bureau of Labor Statistics. The percentage attributed to personal consumption declined with income, and declined sharply with dependents. Thus a single adult earning $10,000 per year was presumed to spend 76.4% of his income on his own consumption, a figure that gradually declined to 48% as income rose to $90,000. If he were married with two dependent children, he was presumed to spend only 13.6% of his income on his own consumption at $10,000 per year, declining to

6.7% as his income rose to $90,000. "For lower income categories where total expenditures exceed income, expenditures were scaled to income, so as not to reduce income for expenses potentially met by other forms of support," such as help from relatives, welfare, food stamps, subsidized housing, and the like. The percentage attributed to the decedent's personal consumption was applied to after-tax income, although BLS apparently calculated it on the basis of before-tax income, and it was applied only to decedent's earnings, although defendants often offer evidence of decedent's personal consumption as a percentage of family income. On each of these points, the Special Master's formula is more favorable to claimants than legal doctrine; it is much harder to compare these calculations to the actual calculations or estimates of a typical jury.

7. Future lost income was discounted to present value using discount rates based on current after-tax yields on "mid- to long-term U.S. Treasury securities," using "a mid-range effective tax rate." It was assumed that the survivors of younger victims would invest in longer term securities, so the discount rates varied with age: 5.1% for victims under age 36 (4.2% after presumed tax), declining to 4.2% (3.4% after presumed tax) for victims over 54. Using mid- to long-term securities increased the discount rate as compared to short-term securities, and thus favored defendant (the government here). Given that the Special Master had already added 2% for projected future inflation, these numbers were at the high end of the 1% to 3% range of real interest rates suggested in *Jones & Laughlin*.

8. The Special Master made other simplifying assumptions "to facilitate analysis on a large scale." Although he projected substantial salary growth over time, he used for each decedent the income-tax rate at the date of death and the personal consumption figures imputed at the date of death. "It was determined that the net effect of these and other facilitating assumptions was to increase the potential amount of presumed economic loss to the benefit of the claimant."

9. To all this, he added a lump sum for "noneconomic loss," subtracted collateral sources very broadly defined, and compared to a de facto guaranteed minimum recovery. These parts of the plan are described in the supplement to page 162.

CHAPTER THREE

PREVENTING HARM:
THE MEASURE OF INJUNCTIVE RELIEF

A. PREVENTIVE INJUNCTIONS

Page 245. After note 7, add:

7.1. The Court took a similar but somewhat different approach in Ayotte v. Planned Parenthood, 546 U.S. 320 (2006). A New Hampshire statute required parental notification before performing an abortion on a minor. The Court has upheld such statutes provided they contain certain exceptions, and the New Hampshire law contained most of the required exceptions. But it did not have an exception for cases where delay would endanger the health of the mother. The lower courts had enjoined all enforcement of the parental notification statute; the Supreme Court suggested it would be more appropriate to enjoin enforcement of the statute only in cases where delay would endanger the mother's health. That much is entirely consistent with *Dalton*.

But the Court did not treat this as a rule derived from the nature of remedies or anything like the rightful position principle. Rather, it was a result derived from somewhat discretionary consideration of three factors. "Generally speaking, when confronting a constitutional flaw in a statute, we try to limit the solution to the problem." *Id.* at 967. "[W]e try not to nullify more of a legislature's work than is necessary." *Id.*

But second, "we restrain ourselves from 'rewrit[ing] state law to conform it to constitutional requirements' even as we strive to salvage it." *Id.* at 968, quoting Virginia v. American Booksellers Association, 484 U.S. 383, 397 (1988). If the governing constitutional law is clearly defined, the court may be able to enter a simple and clear preventive injunction against enforcing the unconstitutional part of the statute. But if the law is not so settled, and crafting a constitutional version of the statute requires legislative judgment, it may be better to enjoin enforcement of the whole statute and leave the drafting of a replacement to the legislature.

And third, "the touchstone for any decision about remedy is legislative intent, for a court cannot 'use its remedial powers to circumvent the intent of the legislature,'" *id.*, quoting Califano v. Westcott, 443 U.S. 76, 94 (1999) (Powell, J., concurring). This sweeping statement is surely overbroad, but the relevant point is sound: legislatures often indicate, in a severability clause or otherwise, whether they would prefer the entire statute or only the invalid portion to be invalidated if part of it is invalid. Usually legislatures prefer the narrower remedy, but if a legislature thinks that part of the statute without the rest would be counterproductive, the court should defer to that intention. These kinds of considerations are not new, and it may be that the *Dalton* Court thought the outcome of any such analysis too obvious to require explanation.

Page 247. At the end of the Note, add:

For a better opinion, more fully explaining the rule in *Hernandez*, see Virginia Society for Human Life, Inc. v. Federal Election Commission, 263 F.3d 379, 392-394 (4th Cir. 2001). For a contrary view, see Justice for All v. Faulkner, 410 F.3d 760 (5th Cir. 2005). The Fifth Circuit seemed to assume that in a case holding a statute or regulation unconstitutional "on its face," as distinguished from holding it unconstitutional in particular applications ("as applied"), the court should enjoin enforcement as to everyone. But the cases it cited in support (in n.16) were First Amendment overbreadth cases, an unusual special context.

Page 250. After note 1, add:

1.1. Most courts have held or assumed that a bona fide claim for nominal damages is enough to avoid mootness, although some of those opinions have expressed doubts. Judge Michael McConnell challenges that assumption in a concurring opinion in Utah Animal Rights Coalition v. Salt Lake City Corp., 371 F.3d 1248 (10th Cir. 2004). He argues that a claim for nominal damages is the functional equivalent of a claim for declaratory judgment, and that both should get similar treatment for mootness purposes. If there is a live dispute between the parties that might be resolved by awarding nominal damages, the case is alive; if not, it is moot. He bowed to contrary circuit authority, but called for en banc or Supreme Court consideration of the issue.

It is an obvious point, but rarely litigated, that a claim for restitution of defendant's unjust gains is never moot. It is always possible to order that those gains be repaid. Laskowski v. Spellings, 443 F.3d 930 (7th Cir. 2006), *vacated on other grounds as* University of Notre Dame v. Laskowski, 2007 WL 1854121 (U.S., June 29, 2007).

Page 251. After note 3 add:

The Court briefly reaffirmed the *Friends of the Earth* standard, and described it as "a heavy burden," in Parents Involved in Community Schools v. Seattle School District No. 1, 2007 WL 1836531 (U.S., June 28, 2007).

Page 259. After note 3, add:

Cheney v. United States District Court, 542 U.S. 367 (2004), the much publicized litigation over disclosure of who advised the Vice President on energy policy, was a mandamus petition to limit allegedly overbroad discovery. The court of appeals said the scope of discovery is discretionary and not reviewable on mandamus; the Supreme Court said it was reviewable on mandamus here, where the Vice President claimed that excessive discovery amounted to judicial interference with the executive branch to an extent inconsistent with the separation of powers. The underlying case was also a mandamus petition, to compel disclosure of certain information.

Page 259. After the second paragraph of note 4, add:

Habeas corpus in its original and most fundamental use is illustrated in Hamdi v. Rumsfeld, 542 U.S. 507 (2004), and Rasul v. Bush, 542 U.S. 466 (2004), both holding that even in the extraordinary conditions of the war on terror, persons held by the executive branch without charges, hearing, or counsel are entitled to some level of judicial review of their detentions.

B. REPARATIVE INJUNCTIONS

Page 264. After note 4, add:

5. There is a more plausible distinction between forward and backward looking remedies in United States v. Philip Morris USA, Inc., 396 F.3d 1190 (D.C. Cir. 2005). This is the government's much publicized racketeering suit against the tobacco companies. The government is suing under the Racketeer Influenced and Corrupt Organizations Act (RICO), 18 U.S.C. §1961 *et seq.* (2000), which appears to authorize criminal penalties in §1963, civil enforcement actions by the government in §1964(a), and private treble damage actions in §1964(c).

Section 1964(a) provides that the federal courts may "prevent and restrain violations." The government sought a form of restitution -- disgorgement of all defendants' profits from sales to persons who had become addicted to nicotine while minors. Restitution and disgorgement are explored in chapter 6. For now, the only question is whether such a recovery would "prevent or restrain violations" of RICO. A divided panel said no. The profits were earned from past violations; paying those profits to the government would do nothing to prevent or restrain future violations. The government relied on United States v. Carson, 52 F.3d 1173 (2d Cir. 1995), which held that disgorgement of profits could prevent future violations to the extent that those profits were being used to fund or promote the illegal conduct or to provide capital for that conduct. The majority in the D.C. Circuit rejected that theory as inconsistent with the statutory structure. It would duplicate the provision in §1963(a)(1) for forfeiture of any interest acquired through a violation, but without the protections of criminal procedure required under §1963. The government also sought compensatory damages, but under other statutes; it apparently did not claim that §1964(a) authorized damages.

Is *Philip Morris* consistent with *American Stores*? I think so. Of course the two statutes are not identical, but each statute authorized remedies aimed at the future. *American Stores* holds that that includes an injunction aimed at preventing the future consequences of a past violation. *Philip Morris* holds that it does not include monetary awards based on past violations.

6. *Philip Morris* is distinguished in United States v. Lane Labs-USA Inc., 427 F.3d 219 (3d Cir. 2005), allowing the government to recover restitution, under the Food, Drug and Cosmetic Act, 21 U.S.C. §301 *et seq.* (2000), of the proceeds from selling a phony cancer cure. That act authorizes federal district courts "to restrain violations," §332(a), but it says nothing about restitution. The court relied on older Supreme Court cases holding that when Congress invokes the courts' equity power to enforce a statutory policy, it means the whole equity power, which includes restitution as well as injunctions. Those cases may be in some tension with more recent Supreme Court cases holding that Congress must spell out the remedies it wants, and that courts cannot imply them. Some of those cases are discussed in *Lane Labs*; others are the subject of section A of chapter 10, in the main volume.

Page 289. After note 15, add:

16. Tracy Thomas argues that prophylactic injunctions are ubiquitous and conceptually simple. Tracy A. Thomas, *The Prophylactic Remedy: Normative Principles and Definitional Parameters of Broad Injunctive Relief*, 52 Buff. L. Rev. 301 (2004). She says prophylactic injunctions are limited by two principles: they must be aimed at the legally cognizable harm identified in the case, not at any other harm; and the factual connection between the prophylactic order and the legally relevant harm "must be sufficiently close to justify the inclusion of the conduct in the court's order," *id.* at 342-343, a requirement she analogizes to proximate cause. Does that help?

C. STRUCTURAL INJUNCTIONS

1. The Scope of the Injunction When Issued

b. Other Examples

Page 312. After note 1, add:

For a conservative critique of the judicial role in prisons, school desegregation, and other contexts, see Stephen P. Powers and Stanley Rothman, *The Least Dangerous Branch? Consequences of Judicial Activism* (Praeger Publishers 2002). Powers and Rothman also provide useful citations to empirical studies of structural litigation.

Page 318. After note 4, add:

5. It is widely assumed that institutional reform litigation peaked long ago and largely disappeared as the federal courts became more conservative. A substantial survey of the cases argues that that is simply not true. Margo Schlanger, *Civil Rights Injunctions Over Time: A Case Study of Jail and Prison Court Orders*, 81 N.Y.U. L. Rev. 550 (2006). She argues that there was essential continuity from the early 1980s to 1996, when the Prison Litigation Reform Act took effect, and that even today, there are more cases than people realize. But the nature of this litigation changed, beginning in the 1980s, in the direction later suggested by Lewis v. Casey: more narrowly targeted complaints, tighter approaches to causation, more rigorous proof. *Lewis* and the PLRA thus confirmed a trend that was already well established.

Page 320. After note 1, add:

For a detailed history of the VMI litigation, from the development of the hazing and lack of privacy policies after World War II, to implementation of the remedy after the Supreme Court's decision, see Philippa Strum, *Women in the Barracks: The VMI Case and Equal Rights* (University Press of Kansas 2002). This is one of a series of Kansas Press studies of prominent Supreme Court cases.

Page 328. At the end of the Note, add:

The district court approved the settlement with one modification -- that the court retain authority to enforce the settlement on its own motion as well as on motion of a party. United States v. Microsoft, 231 F. Supp. 2d 144 (D.D.C. 2002).

2. Modifying Injunctions

Page 342. After note 11, add:

11.1. The Court held unanimously that state officials cannot relitigate the minimum requirements of federal law on plaintiffs' motion to enforce a consent decree. Frew v. Hawkins, 540 U.S. 431 (2004). The reasons the Fifth Circuit held otherwise were based in state sovereign immunity law, taken up in chapter 4, and that part of the case is discussed in more detail in this supplement to page 492.

The consent decree was much more detailed than the federal statute it enforced. The Court said that the state's remedy, if any, was a motion to modify under Rule 60(b)(5). It did not formally amend *Rufo*'s standard, but it had this to say in dictum:

> The federal court must exercise its equitable powers to ensure that when the objects of the decree have been attained, responsibility for discharging the State's obligations is returned to the State and its officials. As public servants, the officials of the State must be presumed to have a high degree of competence in deciding how best to discharge their governmental responsibilities. A State, in the ordinary course, depends upon successor officials, both appointed and elected, to bring new insights and solutions to problems of allocating revenues and resources. The basic obligations of federal law may remain the same, but the precise manner of their discharge may not. If the State establishes reasons to modify the decree, the court should make the necessary changes;

where it has not done so, however, the decree should be enforced according to its terms.

Id. at 441. What reasons must the state establish? Must it be one of the *Rufo* reasons, or does this paragraph create an alternate test? The idea that the injunction may be partly or entirely vacated when it achieves its purpose has been most prominently developed in the school desegregation cases, discussed in the main volume at 345-346.

11.2. The Court in *Frew* said that federal consent decrees "must be directed to protecting federal interests," "must spring from, and serve to resolve, a dispute within the court's subject-matter jurisdiction; must come within the general scope of the case made by the pleadings; and must further the objectives of the law upon which the complaint was based." *Id.* at 437, citing Local No. 93 v. City of Cleveland, 478 U.S. 501, 525 (1986). The context suggests that defendants might be able to raise these limits on a motion to modify or a motion to enforce. But cases in which such a challenge would be successful would surely be quite rare.

Page 345. After note 4, add:

5. There were legislative efforts to generalize some of the more draconian features of the PLRA. The Federal Consent Decree Fairness Act, S.489 and H.R.1229 in the 109th Congress, would have provided that any state or local government or official subject to a consent decree could move to modify or vacate the decree four years after it was entered or whenever a new governor or mayor is elected. On such a motion, "the burden of proof shall be on the party who originally filed the civil action to demonstrate that the continued enforcement of a consent decree is necessary to uphold a Federal right." The decree would lapse if the court did not rule on this motion within 90 days of its filing, and the act would apply to all consent decrees, whether entered before or after its enactment. Hearings were held in both houses in the summer of 2005, but neither bill got out of committee, and they do not appear to have been reintroduced in the 110th Congress.

CHAPTER FOUR

CHOOSING REMEDIES

A. SUBSTITUTIONARY OR SPECIFIC RELIEF

1. Irreplaceable Losses

Page 374. After note 4, add:

5. A far more radical version of the economic argument is suggested in Jeffrey J. Rachlinski and Forest Jourden, *Remedies and the Psychology of Ownership*, 51 Vand. L. Rev. 1541 (1998). A persistent social science finding concerns what has come to be known as the endowment effect: most people demand a higher price to sell something they already own than they would be willing to pay to acquire the thing if they did not own it. The reasons for this effect are more speculative: people become attached to what they own; if owners did not value their property more than most potential buyers, they would have already sold it; people buy and sell in search of gain, so they seek to buy low and sell high; cash is scarce, and people are routinely careful about how they spend it, but they do not routinely sell their possessions to raise more cash. Some of these explanations are potentially more general than others, and quite general explanations are needed. The endowment effect is not universal, but it is very widespread. For example, it seems to appear instantly when experimenters give inexpensive coffee mugs to experimental subjects; it is hard to see how the subjects could have become emotionally attached to the mugs. For a good review of the endowment effect and its implications, see Russell Korobkin, *The Endowment Effect and Legal Analysis*, 97 Nw. U.L. Rev. 1227 (2003).

Rachlinski and Jourden ran an experiment to test whether the endowment effect depends on available remedies. Their findings suggest that the endowment effect disappears if people understand that their property is protected only by liability rules. Some subjects were told that no one can take their property from them unless they agree to sell. Other subjects were told that their property could be taken from them over their objection, and that state law would entitle them to damages. This second group, threatened with involuntary loss of their property, were willing to sell at lower prices, closer to the price they would be willing to pay. This result must be considered tentative, based on only one experiment, but it is certainly plausible.

Assume that Rachlinski and Jourden are empirically right -- that owners will be less attached to their property, and more willing to sell, if they know that anything they own could be taken from them without their consent, at any time, at prices determined by third parties. Here is the surprise: Rachlinski and Jourden think that's a *good* thing. They argue that people's attachment to their property is an irrational barrier to trade, and there would be more purchases and sales if there were universal private eminent domain. They view this as an argument against injunctions to protect property rights, and for confining remedies to liability rules, even in situations where transaction costs are low and the parties could negotiate a sale. 51 Vand. L. Rev. at 1574-1576.

Of course this flies in the face of widespread intuitions about the meaning of ownership. It is equally inconsistent with the general economic preference for voluntary transactions. And it may be that their experimental result does not show less attachment to the property, but simply risk aversion and loss of bargaining power. If my property may be taken at a price I can't control, I may lower my selling price to avoid the risk of receiving even less in a damage award.

Page 383. At the end of the Note, add:

Judge Easterbrook offered a nice example in Campbell v. Miller, 373 F.3d 834 (7th Cir. 2004). To reduce overcrowding in its jails, Indianapolis decided that for certain listed misdemeanors, it would issue a summons and citation instead of taking the suspect into custody. But it authorized the police in such cases to conduct strip and body-cavity searches at the scene, in public. Plaintiff James Campbell, a supervisor for a nearby township, was cited for possession of marijuana and strip searched under this policy, in daylight, in front of a friend's house. No marijuana was found in his possession; no charges were ever brought. The court refused to enjoin the city's policy:

> Campbell supposes that money never is an adequate remedy for a constitutional wrong. That belief is incorrect. Damages are a normal, and adequate, response to an improper search or seizure, which as a constitutional tort often is analogized to (other) personal-injury litigation. Erroneous grants of injunctive relief that hamper enforcement of the criminal law have the potential to cause havoc, while erroneous awards (or denials) of damages to a single person have more limited ability to injure the general public. Judges are fallible, so the costs of false positives always must be considered when choosing among remedies. When the costs of false negatives are low -- and this is what it means to say that the remedy at law is adequate -- there is correspondingly slight reason to incur the risk of premature or overbroad injunctive relief. Campbell's suit is just getting under way, and the City has not had a full opportunity to explain and justify its practices. Once this litigation has run its course, the decision will have precedential effect even if the only remedy is monetary. If this court decides that the City's practice is unconstitutional then it must cease whether or not a formal injunction issues (for the prospect of damages paid to thousands of suspects would bring the City into line). If, however, the City prevails in the end, or suffers only a partial defeat, then avoiding premature injunctive relief will prove to have been a wise exercise of restraint.

Fleshing out the terse aside in the sixth sentence, Easterbrook seems to say that damages are an adequate remedy where the costs of erroneously denying an injunction would be low. There is something to that; it is a way of talking about whether the injunction adds anything important.

Now focus on his main point. Despite the general talk about the higher costs of injunctions, the work in this paragraph is done by "the risk of premature or overbroad injunctive relief" -- not by any differences between injunctive relief that corresponds to the damage remedy. Damages would be awarded to one plaintiff, for one completed search, after a full trial. An injunction to protect that one plaintiff from further similar searches, awarded after a full trial, could not "cause havoc" for anybody. But that is not what Campbell sought or what Easterbrook denied.

Campbell's suit was "just getting under way." He sought a preliminary injunction, based on probabilities, long before any trial. We will take up preliminary injunctions in considerable detail soon; for now, note simply that this request and this procedural change is why the injunction might have been "premature," and why the city might "prevail[] in the end," and the principal reason why the injunction might be erroneous. And Campbell sought to represent a class of all persons arrested for misdemeanors; it is an injunction protecting that whole class that might be "overbroad" and "cause havoc." So it is not that erroneous injunctions have more costs than erroneous awards of damages, but rather that erroneous relief to a large class has more costs than erroneous relief to a single person, and that preliminary relief based on probabilities is more likely to be erroneous than final relief after a full trial.

No class action had been certified; the class was not party to the case. And even if it had been, the court might well have hesitated before universally enjoining the city's policy long before trial and on the sketchiest of records. Campbell himself had shown no likelihood that he would be victimized again. Compare City of Los Angeles v. Lyons, 461 U.S. 95 (1983), summarized in this note in the main volume.

Do any of these considerations mean that damages are an adequate remedy? Of course damages are an adequate remedy for the search Campbell had already suffered; no other remedy is even possible. But injunction cases focus on the future: if the court knew that the police were about to strip search Campbell in public again, should it enjoin the search, or let it happen because damages would be an adequate remedy?

Judge Williams, dissenting, would have issued the preliminary injunction, apparently for the whole uncertified class, although that is unclear. She thought there was ample circuit precedent limiting strip searches (see Levka v. City of Chicago in the main volume at 181), that public strip searches were even worse, that public strip searches were authorized by city policy and appeared to be fairly common, and that experience had shown that damages were little deterrent to police misconduct. She too treated the adequacy of the legal remedy in the abstract, without attending either to the class issue or to the very preliminary stage of the case. Note that both judges treated adequacy of legal remedies largely in terms of deterring defendant, rather than in terms of adequacy for plaintiff.

Page 392. After note 8, add:

9. Steven Shavell proposes a quite different economic analysis in *Specific Performance Versus Damages for Breach of Contract: An Economic Analysis*, 84 Tex. L. Rev. 831 (2006). He assumes that the parties would want to maximize the joint value they derive from the contract, and that remedies can affect this value. In general, he thinks parties to contracts to make something or do something would prefer damages, principally because of the risk that production costs might be unexpectedly high, which might mean that performance would be wasteful or that the parties would engage in wasteful strategic behavior to avoid the costs of performance. The law's response to these sorts of risks is taken up in the next three principal cases. He thinks that parties to contracts to convey property already in existence would prefer specific performance. Here there is no risk of unexpected production costs, and the greater risk is that the seller will breach inefficiently because he underestimates the property's value to the buyer. Of course there are qualifications and elaborations, but that is the heart of it.

He also says that the adequacy of a remedy and the goal of making the victim of breach whole are both irrelevant -- distractions from the true goal of maximizing the joint value of the contract. He assumes that any inadequacy of remedy can always be compensated by an adjustment to the price, an assumption that may be more true in theory than in practice.

10. Melvin Eisenberg offers a powerful attack on the theory of efficient breach, and a powerful refutation of all the economically based attacks on expectancy damages. Melvin A. Eisenberg, *Actual and Virtual Specific Performance, the Theory of Efficient Breach, and the Indifference Principle in Contract Law*, 93 Cal. L. Rev. 975

(2005). Some of his points are highly effective elaborations of points made earlier in the extensive literature, including many of the points in these notes; others appear to be wholly original. He argues that expectancy damages are nearly always inadequate in the real world, and that promisors almost never have information about the value of performance to the promisee -- information that is essential to the theory and that the theory assumes they have. He argues that remedies proposals based on goals other than making the promisee indifferent between performance and compensation -- goals such as adjusting the incentives of the parties or maximizing the joint value of the contract -- are wrongheaded, inadministrable, underdeveloped, mutually inconsistent, and incapable of being made consistent. In his view, "Actual specific performance should be awarded unless a special moral, policy, or experiential reason suggests otherwise in a given class of cases, or the promisee can accomplish virtual specific performance. A promisee can accomplish virtual specific performance if he can readily find in the market a commodity that he could not in good faith reject as an equivalent of the breached performance, given his demonstrable preferences -- by which I mean subjective preferences whose existence can be satisfactorily demonstrated. Cover damages, in turn, should be awarded if a buyer who made a substitute purchase shows that his choice of the covering substitute was made in good faith, given his demonstrable preferences, after he conducted a reasonable search." *Id.* at 978. His examples of "special moral, policy, or experiential reasons" for refusing specific performance are of the sort examined in this rest of this section of the main volume.

2. Burdens on Defendant or the Court

Page 410. After note 4, add:

5. Much of the literature assumes that of course parties will buy their way out of inefficient injunctions, or inefficient refusals to enjoin. That assumption appears to be false. Ward Farnsworth followed up on twenty recent nuisance cases with reported opinions. There was no serious bargaining after judgment in any case, and none of the lawyers believed there would have been bargaining if the

case had come out the other way. In a few cases, there was an initial proposal and a rejection, with no followup from either side; in most cases, there was not even that. The lawyers believed that acrimony from the litigation inhibited bargaining, that winners were unwilling to put a dollar value on what they had won (whether freedom from nuisance or freedom to control the use of their own property), and losers were unwilling to pay bribes to winners. Ward Farnsworth, *Do Parties to Nuisance Cases Bargain After Judgment? A Glimpse Inside the Cathedral*, 66 U. Chi L. Rev. 373 (1999).

The study is small, but its implications are broad. It suggests that the Coase Theorem is at best irrelevant after judgment -- that the law's initial allocation of rights is generally dispositive and parties do not bargain around it. Of course, parties who litigate to judgment may be a special case; this study does not imply that people rarely buy or sell legal entitlements before they get embroiled in litigation. Nor does it necessarily imply anything about settlements after suit is filed and before an opinion is reported. But it may be that the same factors of acrimony and resistance to commodifying intangible rights inhibit settlement of injunction cases, or at least inhibit settlements that reverse that parties' prediction of what the court will do if the case is litigated to judgment.

Professor Coase always said he was talking about a theoretical world with no transaction costs: unless transaction costs interfered, parties would bargain to reallocate rights that the law allocated inefficiently. If high transaction costs are universal in some contexts, Coase is irrelevant to those contexts. But Farnsworth argues that his simple two-party cases with generally modest stakes did not involve high transaction costs. There was no obstacle preventing a deal the parties would have made if they could; rather, neither side wanted to make a deal at all. *Id.* at 406-410. Moreover, he suggests that if we view these litigant preferences merely as a source of transaction costs, the law should try to stamp them out. *Id.* at 422. Compare the proposal to stamp out people's irrational attachments to their property, discussed in the supplement to page 374. But perhaps deep-seated human preferences are values the law should respect and take account of. If human preferences are such that people refuse to bargain even when transaction costs are low, the Coase Theorem may be more wrong than irrelevant. Are acrimony, resistance to commodification, and a general reluctance to bargain just a source of high transaction costs?

Page 418. After note 1, add:

That damage award was eventually reversed on grounds going to liability; the court held that the lease did not require the hospital to remain open for the full term of the lease. Universal Health Services, Inc. v. Renaissance Women's Group, P.A., 121 S.W.3d 742 (Tex. 2003). On our issue, the opinion implies that the trial court eventually concluded, independently of the jury award, that it could not order specific performance.

1.1. Another American case arguably contra is Metropolitan Sports Facilities Commission v. Minnesota Twins Partnership, 638 N.W.2d 214 (Minn. App. 2002), affirming a preliminary injunction ordering the Minnesota Twins to play their 2002 home games at the Hubert H. Humphrey Metrodome near Minneapolis. Major League Baseball had proposed to terminate the franchise, and the Twins claimed they would lose $4 million in the season.

The case is different from *Argyll* in several ways. Only some of these points are relied on in the opinion, which treats the case as rather easy. The contract to play in the Metrodome lasted only one season at a time, and the Twins had renewed that contract in September 2001, only a few weeks before baseball announced its plans to "contract" by eliminating two teams. So any hardship was limited to a single season, not seventeen years, and it was impossible for the Twins to claim that the hardship now anticipated was any different than what they had anticipated when they renewed the contract. In *Argyll*, the store had already closed and removed its fixtures; the Twins had not moved their franchise, released their players, or disbanded their operation.

Moreover, the hardship to the Twins was balanced against a much stronger claim of irreparable injury on plaintiff's side. The Commission collected only nominal rent, and earned about $500,000 per season from a share of concession and advertising revenue. The injury it cared about was the intangible benefits of a major league team to the metropolitan area and its baseball fans. The state supreme court had relied on these benefits when it upheld public

45

financing for the stadium. Major League Baseball, which regularly touts such benefits when it demands such public subsidies on threat of moving franchises, now tried to treat the stadium contract as a simple commercial lease with no public significance. The Commission also found perfect testimony from Bud Selig, the Commissioner of Baseball, explaining that Congress should not repeal baseball's antitrust exemption, lest it "irreparably injure [fans] by leading to the removal of live professional baseball from communities that have hosted major league and minor league teams for decades."

Playing under the mandate of the preliminary injunction, the Twins went on to win their division and the first round of the 2002 post season, before losing to the Angels in the American League Championship Series. In the new collective bargaining agreement, baseball agreed to put off contraction until at least the 2007 season.

Page 421. After note 10, add:

EBAY INC. v. MERCEXCHANGE, L.L.C.
126 S.Ct. 1837 (2006)

Justice THOMAS delivered the opinion of the Court.

Ordinarily, a federal court considering whether to award permanent injunctive relief to a prevailing plaintiff applies the four-factor test historically employed by courts of equity. Petitioners eBay Inc. and Half.com, Inc., argue that this traditional test applies to disputes arising under the Patent Act. We agree and, accordingly, vacate the judgment of the Court of Appeals.

I

Petitioner eBay operates a popular Internet Web site that allows private sellers to list goods they wish to sell, either through an auction or at a fixed price. Petitioner Half.com, now a wholly owned subsidiary of eBay, operates a similar Web site. Respondent MercExchange, L.L.C., holds a number of patents, including a business method patent for an electronic market designed to facilitate the sale of goods between private individuals by establishing a central authority to promote trust among participants. MercExchange sought to license its patent to eBay and Half.com, as it had previously done with other companies, but the parties failed to reach an agreement. MercExchange subsequently filed a patent infringement suit against eBay and Half.com in the United States District Court for the Eastern District of Virginia. A jury found that MercExchange's patent was valid, that eBay and Half.com had infringed that patent, and that an award of damages was appropriate.

Following the jury verdict, the District Court denied MercExchange's motion for permanent injunctive relief. 275 F. Supp. 2d 695 (E.D. Va. 2003). The Court of Appeals for the Federal Circuit reversed, applying its "general rule that courts will issue permanent injunctions against patent infringement absent exceptional circumstances." 401 F.3d 1323, 1339 (Fed. Cir. 2005). We granted certiorari to determine the appropriateness of this general rule.

II

According to well-established principles of equity, a plaintiff seeking a permanent injunction must satisfy a four-factor test before a court may grant such relief. A plaintiff must demonstrate: (1) that it has suffered an irreparable injury; (2) that remedies available at law, such as monetary damages, are inadequate to compensate for that injury; (3) that, considering the balance of hardships between the plaintiff and defendant, a remedy in equity is warranted; and (4) that the public interest would not be disserved by a permanent injunction. *See, e.g.*, Weinberger v. Romero-Barcelo, 456 U.S. 305, 311-13 (1982); Amoco Production Co. v. Gambell, 480 U.S. 31, 42 (1987). The decision to grant or deny permanent injunctive relief is an act of equitable discretion by the district court, reviewable on appeal for abuse of discretion. *See, e.g.*, *Romero-Barcelo*, 456 U.S. at 320.

These familiar principles apply with equal force to disputes arising under the Patent Act. As this Court has long recognized, "a major departure from the long tradition of equity practice should not be lightly implied." *Id.*; *see also* Amoco, 480 U.S. at 542. Nothing in the Patent Act indicates that Congress intended such a departure. To the contrary, the Patent Act expressly provides that injunctions "may" issue "in accordance with the principles of equity." 35 U.S.C. §283 (2000).

To be sure, the Patent Act also declares that "patents shall have the attributes of personal property," §261, including "the right to exclude others from making, using, offering for sale, or selling the invention," §154(a)(1). According to the Court of Appeals, this statutory right to exclude alone justifies its general rule in favor of permanent injunctive relief. But the creation of a right is distinct from the provision of remedies for violations of that right. Indeed, the Patent Act itself indicates that patents shall have the attributes of personal property "[s]ubject to the provisions of this title," §261, including, presumably, the provision that injunctive relief "may" issue only "in accordance with the principles of equity," §283.

This approach is consistent with our treatment of injunctions under the Copyright Act. Like a patent owner, a copyright holder possesses "the right to exclude others from using his property." Fox Film Corp. v. Doyal, 286 U.S. 123, 127 (1932). Like the Patent Act, the Copyright Act provides that courts "may" grant injunctive relief "on such terms as it may deem reasonable to prevent or restrain infringement of a copyright." 17 U.S.C. §502(a) (2000). And as in our decision today, this Court has consistently rejected invitations to replace traditional equitable considerations with a rule that an injunction automatically follows a determination that a copyright has been infringed.

Neither the District Court nor the Court of Appeals below fairly applied these traditional equitable principles in deciding respondent's motion for a permanent injunction. Although the District Court recited the traditional four-factor test, it appeared to adopt certain expansive principles suggesting that injunctive relief could not issue in a broad swath of cases. Most notably, it concluded that a "plaintiff's willingness to license its patents" and "its lack of commercial activity in practicing the patents" would be sufficient to establish that the patent holder would not suffer irreparable harm if an injunction did not issue. 275 F. Supp. 2d at 712. But traditional equitable principles do not permit such broad classifications. For example, some patent holders, such as university researchers or self-made inventors, might reasonably prefer to license their patents, rather than undertake efforts to secure the financing necessary to bring their works to market themselves. Such patent holders may be able to satisfy the traditional four-factor test, and we see no basis for categorically denying them the opportunity to do so. To the extent that the District Court adopted such a categorical rule, then, its analysis cannot be squared with the principles of equity adopted by Congress. The court's categorical rule is also in tension with Continental Paper Bag Co. v. Eastern Paper Bag Co., 210 U.S. 405, 422-30 (1908), which rejected the contention that a court of equity has no jurisdiction to grant injunctive relief to a patent holder who has unreasonably declined to use the patent.

In reversing the District Court, the Court of Appeals departed in the opposite direction from the four-factor test. The court articulated a "general rule," unique to patent disputes, "that a permanent injunction will issue once infringement and validity have been adjudged." 401 F.3d at 1338. The court further indicated that injunctions should be denied only in the "unusual" case, under "exceptional circumstances" and "'in rare instances . . . to protect the public interest.'" Id. at 1338-1339. Just as the District Court erred in its categorical denial of injunctive relief, the Court of Appeals erred in its categorical grant of such relief.

Because we conclude that neither court below correctly applied the traditional four-factor framework that governs the award of injunctive relief, we vacate the judgment of the Court of Appeals, so that the District Court may apply that framework in the first instance. In doing so, we take no position on whether permanent injunctive relief should or should not issue in this particular case, or indeed in any number of other disputes arising under the Patent Act. We hold only that the decision whether to grant or deny injunctive relief rests within the equitable discretion of the district courts, and that such discretion must be exercised consistent with traditional principles of equity, in patent disputes no less than in other cases governed by such standards.

Accordingly, we vacate the judgment of the Court of Appeals, and remand for further proceedings consistent with this opinion.

It is so ordered.

Chief Justice ROBERTS, with whom Justice SCALIA and Justice GINSBURG join, concurring.

I agree with the Court's holding that "the decision whether to grant or deny injunctive relief rests within the equitable discretion of the district courts, and that such discretion must be exercised consistent with traditional principles of equity, in patent disputes no less than in other cases governed by such standards," 126 S.Ct. at 1841, and I join the opinion of the Court. That opinion rightly rests on the proposition that "a major departure from the long tradition of equity practice should not be lightly implied." *Romero-Barcelo*, 456 U.S. at 320.

From at least the early 19th century, courts have granted injunctive relief upon a finding of infringement in the vast majority of patent cases. This "long tradition of equity practice" is not surprising, given the difficulty of protecting a right to exclude through monetary remedies that allow an infringer to use an invention against the patentee's wishes -- a difficulty that often implicates the first two factors of the traditional four-factor test. This historical practice, as the Court holds, does not entitle a patentee to a permanent injunction or justify a general rule that such injunctions should issue. At the same time, there is a difference between exercising equitable discretion pursuant to the established four-factor test and writing on an entirely clean slate. "Discretion is not whim, and limiting discretion according to legal standards helps promote the basic principle of justice that like cases should be decided alike." Martin v. Franklin Capital Corp., 546 U.S. 132 (2005). When it comes to discerning and applying those standards, in this area as others, "a page of history is worth a volume of logic." New York Trust Co. v. Eisner, 256 U.S. 345, 349 (1921) (opinion for the Court by Holmes, J.).

Justice KENNEDY, with whom Justice STEVENS, Justice SOUTER, and Justice BREYER join, concurring.

The Court is correct, in my view, to hold that courts should apply the well-established, four-factor test -- without resort to categorical rules -- in deciding whether to grant injunctive relief in patent cases. THE CHIEF JUSTICE is also correct that history may be instructive in applying this test. The traditional practice of issuing injunctions against patent infringers, however, does not seem to rest on "the difficulty of protecting a right to exclude through monetary remedies that allow an infringer to use an invention against the patentee's wishes." 126 S.Ct. at 1841 (ROBERTS, C.J., concurring). Both the terms of the Patent Act and the traditional view of injunctive relief accept that the existence of a right to exclude does not dictate the remedy for a violation of that right. To the extent earlier cases establish a pattern of granting an injunction against patent infringers almost as a matter of course, this pattern simply illustrates the result of the four-factor test in the contexts then prevalent. The lesson of the historical practice, therefore, is most helpful and instructive when the circumstances of a case bear substantial parallels to litigation the courts have confronted before.

In cases now arising trial courts should bear in mind that in many instances the nature of the patent being enforced and the economic function of the patent holder present considerations quite unlike earlier cases. An industry has developed in which firms use patents not as a basis for producing and selling goods but, instead, primarily for obtaining licensing fees. For these firms, an injunction, and the potentially serious sanctions arising from its violation, can be employed as a bargaining tool to charge exorbitant fees to companies that seek to buy licenses to practice the patent. When the patented invention is but a small component of the product the companies seek to produce and the threat of an injunction is employed simply for undue leverage in negotiations, legal damages may well be sufficient to compensate for the infringement and an injunction may not serve the public interest. In addition injunctive relief may have different consequences for the burgeoning number of patents over business methods, which were not of much economic and legal significance in earlier times. The potential vagueness and suspect validity of some of these patents may affect the calculus under the four-factor test.

The equitable discretion over injunctions, granted by the Patent Act, is well suited to allow courts to adapt to the rapid technological and legal developments in the patent system. For these reasons it should be recognized that district courts must determine whether past practice fits the circumstances of the cases before them. With these observations, I join the opinion of the Court.

NOTES ON CONFUSION IN THE SUPREME COURT

1. The majority opinion has potential for enormous mischief unless -- and possibly even if -- it is read in light of the concurring opinions on behalf of seven justices who believe that the Court's four-factor test generally leads to issuing the injunction. Certainly the grant of a permanent injunction is not automatic on a showing of liability. But there is no "familiar" four-factor test; if the Court has ever announced such a test before, I do not know where it appears, and the Court does not cite it. And in conversations with several other remedies scholars, I found no one who believes there was ever such a test.

2. The Court cites two cases for its four-factor test, *Romero-Barcelo* and *Amoco*. Both are preliminary injunction cases, not permanent injunction cases. Preliminary injunctions are issued before a final decision on the merits, and as we shall see in chapter 4B, that is an important distinction. In preliminary injunction cases, there is indeed a familiar four-part test, although neither *Romero-Barcelo* nor *Amoco* actually recites it.

3. Irreparable injury is a traditional prerequisite to injunctive relief, although as we have seen, irreparable injury is usually easy to show at the stage of permanent injunctions. The Court adds no-adequate-remedy-at-law as a second element of its test, once again suggesting that this is something distinct from irreparable injury and once again giving not the slightest hint what the difference might be. In the "familiar" four-part test for preliminary injunctions, one element is probability of success on the merits. That would make no sense as applied to permanent injunctions, which are issued after success on the merits has been established. It might have been sensible to substitute actual success for probable success, but instead, the Court divided irreparable injury into two elements to get back to four parts in its test.

4. Undue hardship and collateral consequences for the public interest can both be reasons to withhold an injunction, but each is unusual. Certainly it makes no sense to require plaintiff to "demonstrate" all four elements of this test, implying that plaintiff must raise the issues of undue hardship and public interest and

negate them in every case. Undue hardship makes more sense as a defense, with the burden on the guilty defendant to show sufficient hardship to justify excusing him from complying with the law or undoing the consequences of his past violation.

5. The only hint of what should have been the real issue in *eBay* comes in the penultimate paragraph of Justice Kennedy's concurring opinion. Plaintiff claimed patents on some forms of the idea of being an intermediary between buyers and sellers on the Internet, although it had never developed a successful business based on that patent. After eBay's commercial success, plaintiff claimed that its patents covered important parts of eBay's operation. More generally, high-tech industries have been plagued by dormant patents, or what's worse, dormant patent applications, that are allowed to lie fallow until they can be raised to assert a claim to essential parts of a substantial business developed by someone else. The threat of shutting down eBay, or Blackberries, or any other lucrative business, gives enormous bargaining leverage. These cases easily fit the pattern of classic undue hardship cases; defendant has invested much money and effort and now must pay ransom or destroy or abandon his investment. It should not matter whether that investment was in a building or a business. If defendant was not reckless with regard to plaintiff's patent rights, the undue hardship defense readily applies.

6. Some of the nation's most distinguished lawyers litigated *eBay*, but no remedies specialists were involved, and remedies scholars didn't see the case coming until it was too late to file amicus briefs. The briefs talked about demands for excessive licensing fees based on the terrible threat of shutting down much of defendant's operation, but that point was not the core of the argument, and it was never put in the context of the undue hardship defense. As a result, we may be stuck for the indefinite future with an ill-conceived four-part test that generates a lot of wasted effort and confusion as it clumsily reaches the result that would have been reached without it.

3. Reasons of Substantive or Procedural Policy

Page 431. After note 6, add:

6.1. Celebrity lawyer Johnny Cochran was the plaintiff in a case that was like *Willing* only worse. Cochran v. Tory, 544 U.S. 734 (2005). In 1983, Tory retained Cochran to represent him in a claim against the City of Los Angeles for personal injuries suffered in a shoot out with the police. In 1985, Tory accused Cochran of conspiring against his client and promised not to go public with these allegations if Cochran paid him $10 million. Cochran withdrew from the case and collected nothing on his contingent fee contract. In 1995, when Cochran was much in the news because of his role in the pervasively publicized murder trial of O.J. Simpson, Tory demanded that Cochran refund money Tory had paid to another lawyer who had once been loosely associated with Cochran. Cochran did not respond.

Finally, in the late 1990s, Tory and "a troop of people" began picketing outside Cochran's office and outside the Los Angeles Superior Court. They carried signs accusing Cochran of all sorts of wrongdoing. Tory apparently recruited homeless picketers by giving them a ride and buying them lunch. The trial judge found that the statements were false, that Tory knew they were false, and that they were made "for the purpose of inducing Cochran to pay Tory various amounts of money to which Tory was not entitled." He enjoined Tory and anyone cooperating with him from making any written or oral statements about Cochran or his law firm in any public forum. The court of appeals affirmed, relying on *Aguilar* for the proposition that the rule against prior restraints is a rule against restraints prior to a final adjudication that the speech is unprotected.

Cochran died after argument in the Supreme Court, and his widow was substituted as plaintiff. The Court held that the case was not moot, because under California law, the injunction appeared to continue in effect and thus to restrain Tory's speech. But the injunction had lost all or much of its underlying rationale; Tory could no longer hope to coerce payments from Cochran by picketing Cochran's law office. Either the injunction was no longer needed, or it was an overbroad prior restraint. Cochran's widow remained free to seek a narrower injunction in the California courts. But we lost an opportunity for a Supreme Court clarification of the prior restraint rule after final judgment.

Page 439. After note 5, add:

5.1. Another obvious exception is Ashcraft & Gerel v. Coady, in the main volume at page 83, enforcing a liquidated damage clause against a departing law partner. I have no excuse for missing that connection. A similar example is Miami Dolphins, Ltd. v. Williams, 356 F. Supp. 2d 1301 (S.D. Fla. 2005). Ricky Williams, the college hero and Heisman Trophy winner who has behaved erratically in the pros, abruptly quit the Dolphins on the eve of the 2004 season. His contract expressly provided for the pro rata return of his signing bonus and the return of all his incentive bonuses if he quit, refused to practice, or was "otherwise in breach of this Contract." An arbitrator awarded $8.6 million to the Dolphins, apparently accepting the Dolphins' argument that Florida restrictions on penalty clauses did not apply to these provisions. The federal court enforced the award, noting the federal policy of deference to arbitration under collective bargaining agreements.

B. PRELIMINARY OR PERMANENT RELIEF

Page 445. After note 2, add:

2.1. See the discussion of the *Minnesota Twins* case in this supplement to page 418. The court there easily found irreparable injury, even at the preliminary injunction stage, by focusing on the harm to fans rather than lost revenue to the stadium. Unlike the *Coliseum* court, the *Twins* court had no difficulty considering irreparable harm to third parties or the public. Other factors also helped: probability of success was much higher on a suit to enforce an unambiguous contract than on a novel antitrust claim; the *Twins* court was keeping the Twins where they had been for forty years, but plaintiff in *Coliseum* sought a preliminary injunction to move the Raiders to a place they had never been; the Raiders could move a year or two later if they prevailed, but the plan in *Twins* was to terminate the franchise and break up the team, so that denial of a preliminary injunction would likely have made a permanent injunction impossible. These factors undoubtedly affected the court's intuitive reaction to the case, even though they appear only tangentially (at most) in the opinion.

Page 445. After note 4, add:

4.1. The Court has affirmed a preliminary injunction against enforcement of the Child Online Protection Act, 47 U.S.C. §231 (2000), which regulates pornography on the Internet. Ashcroft v. ACLU, 542 U.S. 656 (2004). The opinion does not recite the four factors, and it says nothing explicit about whether the factors are to be balanced or satisfied separately. It finds probability of success, irreparable injury, and balance of hardships favoring plaintiff, and it discusses a number of "important practical reasons" for its decision. So there was not much to balance in the majority's view, but the list of practical points outside the canonical list of four factors strongly implies an all-things-considered balancing approach.

The district judge found the statute probably unconstitutional because he thought that filters on home computers were a less restrictive means of protecting children. The heart of the Supreme Court's opinion is about the government's prospects of rebutting that preliminary finding. This makes it a nice citation in response to the wrongheaded claim, occasionally found in lower court opinions, that consideration of affirmative defenses is irrelevant to the probability of success at the preliminary injunction stage. For more on *Ashcroft*, see the supplement to 475.

4.2. The point about affirmative defenses is repeated in Gonzales v. O Centro Espirita Beneficiente Uniao Do Vegetal v. Ashcroft, 546 U.S. 418 (2006), affirming a preliminary injunction under the Religious Freedom Restoration Act, 42 U.S.C. §2000bb *et seq.* (2000). Plaintiffs showed a substantial burden on their religion; the burden of proof then shifted to the government to show that that burden was necessary to serve a compelling government interest. On the compelling interest issue, the trial court found the evidence "in equipoise." It followed that the government had not carried its burden on the affirmative defense of compelling interest, and thus that based on the evidence at the preliminary injunction hearing, plaintiffs would probably succeed on the merits. As the court summarized, "the burdens at the preliminary injunction stage track the burdens at trial." 126 S.Ct. at 1218. For more on *O Centro*, see the supplement to 450.

Page 450. After note 6, add:

7. The significance of the status quo was emphatically reaffirmed in O Centro Espirita Beneficente Uniao Do Vegetal v. Ashcroft, 389 F.3d 973 (10th Cir. 2004) (en banc), *aff'd on other grounds*, 546 U.S. 418 (2006). Seven judges, in opinions by Judge Murphy and Judge McConnell, reaffirmed a Tenth Circuit rule that three categories of preliminary injunctions -- preliminary injunctions changing the status quo, mandatory preliminary injunctions, and preliminary injunctions granting all the relief that could be granted at trial -- are "disfavored." Requests for such injunctions "must be more closely scrutinized to assure that the exigencies of the case support the granting of a remedy that is extraordinary even in the normal course." Plaintiff "must make a strong showing both with regard to the likelihood of success on the merits and with regard to the balance of harms," and may not rely on a sliding scale of the sort described in *Coliseum*. 389 F.3d at 975-976 (per curiam).

The seven judges in the majority squarely deny that preliminary injunctions are exclusively, or even primarily, about minimizing the risk of erroneously inflicted irreparable injury. Judge Murphy, writing for all seven judges, insists that "the underlying purpose of the preliminary injunction is to 'preserve the relative positions of the parties until a trial on the merits can be held,'" quoting University of Texas v. Camenisch, 451 U.S. 390, 395 (1981). He also argues that a court is responsible for erroneously inflicted harm when it changes the status quo, but not when it refuses to change the status quo.

Judge McConnell, in a longer and more thoughtful opinion for four of the seven, argued that preserving the status quo cannot be reduced to minimizing irreparable injury. He collected older cases and treatises that emphasized the importance of the status quo, citing these as evidence of "traditional equity practice." *Id.* at 1012. He argued that emphasis on the status quo followed from appropriate caution in the face of uncertainty and simply from people's attachment to it. "Notwithstanding the tendency of those trained in economics to view opportunity costs as equivalent to actual expenditures, modern social science research has confirmed the reality of 'loss aversion' (the tendency to attach greater value to losses than to foregone gains of equal amount), and the closely related 'endowment effect' (the tendency to value already possessed goods more than prospective acquisitions)." *Id.* at 1016. He argued that the status quo goes to the parties' credibility; plaintiff's claim of irreparable injury is dubious if he has tolerated the status quo for a long time. Preserving the status quo is some check on strategic behavior after the dispute arises.

> Without a heightened standard, these concerns will likely not be given due weight. In the context of the balance of harms analysis, it is all too easy to stop at comparing the absolute magnitudes of the parties' irreparable harms, without distinguishing between foregone gains and actual losses, and without considering whether granting an injunction implicates other institutional concerns about the proper role of the courts. Unless the district court self-consciously takes the nature of the injunction into account by applying a heightened standard, the four factors likely will lead to an overconfident approach to preliminary relief, increasing the cost and disruption from improvidently granted preliminary injunctions.

Id. at 1018. Judge McConnell argued that injunctions reversing recent changes to the status quo were not an exception, but simply injunctions to restore the true status quo. And he accepted decisions in every circuit holding that "there are cases in which preservation of the status quo may so clearly inflict irreparable harm on the movant, with so little probability of being upheld on the merits, that a preliminary injunction may be appropriate even though it requires a departure from the status quo." *Id.* at 1013. Indeed, he voted to affirm the preliminary injunction in the case before him, in part because plaintiff relied on a statute that expressly placed the burden of proof on the government, and the government had not carried its burden.

Judge Seymour, for six judges dissenting on the status quo issue, argued that "the very purpose of preserving the status quo by the grant of a preliminary injunction is to prevent irreparable harm pending a trial on the merits." *Id.* at 1001. And she quoted Professor Dobbs' explanation of the Posner-Leubsdorf standard. But even she conceded that the majority's heightened standard should apply to mandatory preliminary injunctions and injunctions granting all the relief that could be granted at trial.

Most mandatory injunctions will change the status quo, but in this case, the two categories arguably diverged. Plaintiff in *O Centro* is a church that uses in its worship services an herbal tea that contains a mild hallucinogenic agent. The chemical with the hallucinogenic effect is an illegal Schedule I drug. So the church sought a simple preventive injunction against enforcement of the federal drug laws as applied to its worship services. But in the majority's view, preventing enforcement of the drug laws would change the status quo.

The judges also disagreed over the status quo. Judge Seymour saw "two plausible status quos." *Id.* at 1007. The church had in fact been using the tea in its worship for years; for the church, the status quo was undisturbed worship. For the government, the status quo was that it was enforcing the law. These two status quos had coexisted because the church had worshiped in secret and imported the tea clandestinely; when the government found out, it moved to seize shipments of tea in transit. Judge Seymour did not try to choose between these competing status quos; she turned instead to the irreparable harms that would be inflicted on each side. The majority thought the last peaceable, uncontested status quo could not be a condition that existed only in secret.

One irony of *O Centro* is that the district court held a two-week preliminary injunction hearing after allowing the parties a year to prepare. It is not at all clear that any additional evidence the parties may offer at a final trial will add much, or change the district court's fact finding. Nor is it surprising that the district judge was reluctant to enjoin enforcement of the drug laws, even in one narrow application, without giving the government a full chance to make its case. So uncertainty may be quite limited here. If the court had consolidated the preliminary injunction hearing with the trial on the merits, as authorized by Rule 65(a)(2), we might have gotten the same evidence and the same result, but cast as a final judgment instead of a preliminary injunction, thus avoiding this whole controversy over heightened standards and uncertainty. For more on *O Centro*, see supplement to 447.

8. The status quo also played a big role in In re Newton, 146 S.W.3d 648 (Tex. 2004), although there were many grounds for decision in that case. Texas opens a limited number of polling places for "early voting" two weeks before the election. On October 18, 2004, the first day of early voting, a district court issued a temporary restraining order prohibiting a principal Republican political action committee (PAC) from expending any funds raised from unions or corporations. The judge set a preliminary injunction hearing for November 3, the day after the election.

The state supreme court unanimously issued a writ of mandamus directing the judge to vacate the TRO. The court agreed that "the continuation of illegal conduct cannot be justified as preservation of the status quo," but "neither should conduct be adjudicated illegal based merely on the pleadings and a brief, non-evidentiary TRO hearing when substantial rights are involved and the issues are far from clear." *Id.* at 651. The merits were unclear (which goes to probability of success), and defendants made substantial assertions of free speech rights (which goes both to probability of success and balance of hardships). "The plaintiffs assert that violations have been ongoing for years, but nothing in their pleadings suggests a legitimate reason for the plaintiffs to have delayed raising these issues until the day before early voting started." *Id.* at 652. "Under these circumstances, the status quo to be preserved is that of ART PAC's publicly reported and until now unchallenged activities over the past four years." *Id.* By granting the TRO and setting the next hearing for after the election, "the district court has essentially made a final, non-appealable adjudication." *Id.*

Page 475. After the first paragraph of note 10, add:

The single Justice will sometimes rule without referring the motion to the full Court. My impression -- no more than that, because I have not been counting cases -- is that this is becoming more common, and referrals less common. Two examples, issued on election day 2004 and refusing to stay orders of the court of appeals in disputes about eligibility to vote, are Spencer v. Pugh, 543 U.S. 1301 (2004) (Stevens, J.), and Democratic National Committee v. Republican National Committee, 543 U.S. 1304 (2004) (Souter, J.). An example where the Justice just seemed to think the case was easy is Multimedia Holdings Corp. v. Circuit Court, 544 U.S. 1301 (2005) (Kennedy, J.), refusing to stay an order that by its terms did not apply to the party seeking the stay. In Doe v. Gonzales, 546 U.S. 1301 (2005), Justice Ginsburg refused to vacate a stay entered by the court of appeals, without consulting the rest of the Court. The district court had preliminarily enjoined enforcement of a provision of the Patriot Act; Justice Ginsburg's opinion is also notable for its reliance on information under seal and redacted from the published version of her opinion.

On the other hand, in Purcell v. Gonzales, 127 S.Ct. 5 (2006), Justice Kennedy referred the motion to the full Court, and the Court did not simply sign off on his proposed resolution; it issued a per curiam opinion, vacating the injunction pending appeal issued by the court of appeals and reinstating the district court's order refusing a preliminary injunction.

Page 475. After note 11, add:

11.1. The point is dramatically illustrated in Ashcroft v. ACLU, 542 U.S. 656 (2004), affirming a preliminary injunction against a statute regulating Internet porn. The Court emphasizes that preliminary injunction decisions are reviewed for abuse of discretion, and draws the inference that if the case is close, it should affirm. The preliminary injunction was issued in 1999, affirmed by the court of appeals in 2000, vacated and remanded to the court of appeals in 2002, reaffirmed by the court of appeals in 2003, affirmed by the Supreme Court in 2004 on the ground that the case is at least close, and now remanded to the district court for further fact finding. It is a safe bet that the Court as it was composed in 2004 would invalidate the statute unless the government finds better evidence on why filters don't work, so the parties have learned something. And the plaintiffs got five years of protection from the statute. But five years of litigation has not determined whether the statute is constitutional.

C. PROSPECTIVE OR RETROSPECTIVE RELIEF

1. Suits Against Officers in Their Official Capacities

Page 485. After note 9, add:

9.1 The Court relied on the in rem theory in Tennessee Student Assistance Corp. v. Hood, 541 U.S. 440 (2004), to hold that bankruptcy courts can discharge student loans owed to states. The Court said that the bankruptcy court's jurisdiction is based on in rem jurisdiction over the bankrupt estate, not on personal jurisdiction over the creditors.

Tennessee conceded that debts owed to states were generally dischargeable, but it argued that student loans were different. Responding to stories of students cynically discharging their student loans shortly after graduation, and before acquiring any assets, Congress required bankrupt debtors to secure a determination that not discharging their student loans would impose "undue hardship." To request such a determination, the debtor must file an adversary proceeding against the state. Justices Thomas and Scalia, dissenting, said this was equivalent to suing the state. The majority said it was like filing a motion within the in rem bankruptcy proceeding.

9.2. The Court extended *Hood* in Central Virginia Community College v. Katz, 546 U.S. 356 (2006). The bankrupt debtor operated college bookstores at multiple campuses. The debtor's trustee in bankruptcy sued four state colleges to recover preferential transfers -- payments, in the last ninety days before bankruptcy, of debts owed to the colleges (thus preferring the colleges over other unpaid creditors). This is an important step beyond *Hood*, because in *Katz* the trustee sought to recover money from the state colleges, and not merely to resolve issues concerning the college's claims against the debtor.

Seminole Tribe had said broadly that Congress cannot use Article I powers to override state immunity. Hoffman v. Connecticut Dept. of Income Maintenance, 492 U.S. 96 (1989), had said that bankruptcy courts lacked jurisdiction to recover preferential transfers from states, either because Congress had not authorized such recoveries with sufficiently plain language (the plurality), or because Congress lacked power to override state immunity for this purpose (Scalia and O'Connor, JJ., in separate concurring opinions). But in *Katz*, Justice O'Connor joined Stevens, Souter, Ginsburg, and Breyer to reach the opposite result, rejecting the earlier statements as erroneous and dictum. Bankruptcy jurisdiction is "chiefly *in rem* -- a narrow jurisdiction that does not implicate state sovereignty to nearly the same degree as other kinds of jurisdiction." 126 S.Ct. at 1005. And bankruptcy jurisdiction includes claims that are at least arguably in personam but ancillary and "necessary to effectuate the *in rem* jurisdiction of the bankruptcy courts." *Id.* Interstate conflicts over bankruptcy were a problem at the founding, the Convention authorized a uniform federal law of bankruptcy, and adjudicating the rights of states in bankruptcy courts simply did not trigger the founding generation's concern with state sovereignty. To the extent the states had any rights of sovereign immunity in bankruptcy, those rights were surrendered "in the plan of the Convention," and the power to recover preferential transfers from states does not depend on any express Congressional declaration abrogating state sovereign immunity. Justices Roberts, Scalia, Kennedy, and Thomas dissented in a vigorous opinion by Justice Thomas.

The trustee also had claims to recover accounts receivable from some of the state colleges. These claims would seem to be covered by the reasoning in *Katz*, but that issue was not reached; the trustee hedged his bets in the Supreme Court by abandoning those claims.

Page 486. After note 10, add:

11. Ex parte Young got a vigorous reaffirmation and application in Verizon Maryland, Inc. v. Public Service Commission, 535 U.S. 635 (2002). The Maryland Public Service Commission decided a question of federal law about the regulation of certain contracts among providers of telecommunication services. Verizon sued the members of the Commission in their official capacity in federal district court, seeking an injunction against future enforcement of the Commission's order and a declaratory judgment that the order was ineffective both as to the present and as to the past. The Fourth Circuit dismissed, and the Supreme Court unanimously reversed.

Justice Scalia wrote the opinion. An Ex parte Young action may proceed if the "complaint alleges an ongoing violation of federal law and seeks relief properly characterized as prospective," quoting the concurring opinion in *Coeur d'Alene* and also citing the dissent, thus collecting seven Justices who supported that proposition in *Coeur d'Alene*. This was such a case. The Court noted that *Young* itself had effectively been an appeal from the decision of a state regulatory commission. The declaratory judgment as to the past would impose no monetary liability on the state; its purpose was to create a basis for imposing monetary liability on other private parties.

Justice Kennedy joined the opinion, but also filed a short concurrence reasserting his view that "our Ex parte Young jurisprudence requires careful consideration of the sovereign interests of the State as well as the obligations of state officials to respect the supremacy of federal law." *Id.* at 649. He thought this consideration had been implicit in earlier cases, and that without it, "the Eleventh Amendment, and not Ex parte Young, would become the legal fiction." *Id.* Justices Souter, Ginsburg, and Breyer, who also joined the Court's opinion, wrote separately to say that this was just a form of appeal from the Commission's order, and not a suit against the state at all, so that the Eleventh Amendment was not even implicated.

Page 491. After note 12, add:

12.1. The Court has upheld retrospective remedies against a state under the Family and Medical Leave Act, 29 U.S.C. §2601 *et seq.* (2000). Nevada Department of Human Resources v. Hibbs, 538 U.S. 721 (2003). The opinion found a pattern of sex discrimination that Congress could address under the Fourteenth Amendment by requiring uniform family leaves for all workers. The opinion is notably more deferential to Congress than the earlier cases in this series.

12.2. Note 12 of the main volume says the Court invalidated retrospective remedies against states under the Americans with Disabilities Act. Shorthand is dangerous; a more accurate statement would have specified Title I of that Act. Title I regulates employment; it requires reasonable accommodation of disabled but qualified workers.

The Court has now upheld retrospective remedies against states under some applications of Title II of the Act. Tennessee v. Lane, 541 U.S. 509 (2004). Title II regulates access to public services, programs, and activities. The majority focused on access to courthouses, the particular application of the act at issue in *Lane*. Lane refused to crawl up two flights of stairs, or to be carried by deputies, to appear at a hearing in a criminal case; he was arrested and jailed for failure to appear. The Court held that there is a constitutional right of access to criminal trials, that access to criminal justice sometimes requires affirmative efforts or expenditures by states (citing the rights to counsel and to transcripts), and that the ADA as applied to courthouses reasonably enforced that right. Justice O'Connor joined the usual four dissenters to make the majority. Chief Justice Rehnquist, and Justices Scalia, Kennedy, and Thomas, all dissenting here, appeared to think the case was not even close.

12.3. The Court has unanimously held that Congress can override state immunity on statutory claims to the extent that the facts alleged in support of those claims would also support constitutional violations. United States v. Georgia, 546 U.S. 151 (2006). (Despite the case caption, the case concerned Georgia's claimed immunity from suit by a private plaintiff. The United States intervened on appeal to defend the constitutionality of the federal statute authorizing private suits for damages.) The private plaintiff was a paraplegic who alleged that he was confined 23 hours a day in a cell so narrow that he could not turn his wheelchair. He alleged that the shower, the toilet, and his bed were all inaccessible without assistance, and that the guards often refused to assist him. The Eleventh Circuit held that these allegations stated claims under the Eighth Amendment, but dismissed parallel claims under Title II of the Americans with Disability Act on grounds of sovereign immunity.

To the extent that the constitutional and statutory claims are identical, one may wonder when the Supreme Court's holding will matter. Section 1983 would provide a cause of action on the constitutional claims, and §1988 would authorize attorneys' fees. There may be cases where the statutory claim provides some additional remedy, or a helpful procedural or evidentiary rule. There may be cases where Congressional codification of a right focuses judicial attention and facilitates proof and persuasion. And of course there may be cases where the statutory claim closely parallels the constitutional claim but expands it slightly. Those cases would not appear to fall within the rule of United States v. Georgia, but that rule may provide the starting point for the argument that such minor increments to the scope of constitutional protection are within the scope of Congress's ill-defined power to enact prophylactic enforcement rules that are "congruent" and "proportionate" to the underlying constitutional right.

12.4. See also notes 9.1 and 9.2 in the supplement to page 485, explaining the emerging bankruptcy exception to state sovereign immunity.

Page 492. After note 13, add:

13.1. The *Alden* immunity in state court is an immunity from federal claims. States do not have federal immunity from suit in the courts of a sister state, and the forum state does not owe full faith and credit to the immunity rules of the defendant state. Nevada v. Hall, 440 U.S. 410 (1979). The full-faith-and-credit half of this proposition was unanimously reaffirmed in Franchise Tax Board v. Hyatt, 538 U.S. 488 (2003).

How does a state get itself sued in the courts of a sister state? In *Hall*, an employee of the University of Nevada drove a state vehicle into California and into a collision. In *Hyatt*, Hyatt claimed to be a Nevada resident and California tax authorities claimed he was a California resident. He sued in Nevada for a declaratory judgment of his residence, and for damages from intentional torts allegedly committed in the vigorous investigation. Note that California had exercised jurisdiction over Nevada in *Hall*, and then insisted that Nevada could not exercise jurisdiction over California.

Page 492. After note 14, add:

14.1. States are immune from quasi-judicial proceedings before federal administrative agencies. Federal Maritime Commission v. South Carolina State Ports Authority, 535 U.S. 743 (2002). There were the usual four dissents.

The significance of the case is unclear. A private party filed a complaint against the Ports Authority with the Commission, seeking an order requiring future compliance with federal law and reparations for the past. This looks like an injunction, permitted under *Edelman*, and damages, prohibited under *Edelman*, but the Court said the proceeding was inconsistent with the dignity of the state and that all forms of relief were barred. The Court did not explain, but the only explanation in light of past decisions is that all forms of relief were barred because the state agency was named in the case caption. See Alabama v. Pugh, 438 U.S. 781 (1978), granting certiorari to reverse an injunction against the State of Alabama, leaving in place an identical injunction against numerous state officials.

What other remedies are available, and whether complaining parties can name state officials as respondents before administrative agencies, probably depends on substantive and procedural rules at each agency. In the case before the Court, it appeared that adequate injunctive remedies were available if the Commission chose to pursue them, and of course the complaining party can lobby the Commission informally even if it cannot file a formal proceeding. It also appeared that damage remedies were unavailable however this case came out, because the complaining party would have to sue the state to enforce any money order from the Commission. That suit would be barred by the Eleventh Amendment, and Congress has not authorized the Commission to sue to recover money for private parties.

Page 492. After note 15, add:

15.1. A state can also waive its immunity in open court, one case at a time. And the Court has generally held that when a state voluntarily invokes the jurisdiction of a federal court, it waives immunity to any claim that may be asserted against it in that proceeding. The recent invigoration of immunity doctrine had cast doubt on that doctrine, and the Court had to reaffirm it in Lapides v. Board of Regents, 535 U.S. 613 (2002). The case became the occasion to clear up another long-standing anomaly.

Lapides filed state and federal claims against the University of Georgia and its administrative officials in both their personal and official capacities. He filed in state court. Defendants removed the case to federal court, and then moved to dismiss on grounds of various immunities, including the university's Eleventh Amendment immunity. The Eleventh Circuit approved this maneuver; the Supreme Court unanimously reversed. When the university removed the case to federal court, it waived its Eleventh Amendment immunity. The Court said that waivers in litigation were a matter of litigation fairness, to be determined by objective federal rules, and that they did not depend on state law, clear statements, or a grant of authority to the state attorney general. The decision is formally limited to the state-law claims, because the Supreme Court also held that Lapides had stated no federal claim against the university, but the Court's reasoning would plainly apply to federal claims as well, as the courts of appeals have so held. The cases are collected in Meyers v. Texas, 410 F.3d 236 (5th Cir. 2005). Resistance continues; *Meyers* introduces the bizarre notion that Texas might still be immune from *liability* under state law even though it has waived its immunity from *suit* under federal law, and it leaves that issue to be resolved on remand to the district court. And *Lapides* held open the possibility that the United States might be able to remove cases to federal court without waiving anything.

Lapides overrules one of the holdings in an old chestnut, Ford Motor Co. v. Department of Treasury, 323 U.S. 459, 466-470 (1945). In *Ford*, the state defended the lawsuit on the merits in the district court and court of appeals, lost in both courts, and then asserted the Eleventh Amendment for the first time in the Supreme Court. Any other defense would have been waived by the failure to raise it in the lower courts, but the Court said the Eleventh Amendment was too fundamental to be waived by mere silence. Justice Kennedy had criticized *Ford* as letting states litigate without risk. If they win they get the benefits of res judicata (and a favorable precedent); if they lose, they could still assert immunity. Wisconsin Department of Corrections v. Schacht, 524 U.S. 381, 394 (1998) (concurring). No more; this part of *Ford* has been overruled, and the Eleventh Amendment can be waived by failing to raise it.

Edelman explained the *Ford* rule on the ground that the Eleventh Amendment is somewhat like a rule of subject matter jurisdiction. Subject matter jurisdiction can be raised at any time, but the risk of raising the issue late is distributed evenly, because either side can raise it and the court is obliged to raise it on its own motion and, if necessary, to dismiss over the objection of both parties. The court has never been obliged to enforce the Eleventh Amendment if the state wants to waive it, and Justice Kennedy suggested in *Schacht* that the Eleventh Amendment might be better understood as a rule about jurisdiction over the person of the state; a defendant can always consent to personal jurisdiction.

15.2. The Court held unanimously that the Eleventh Amendment does not bar the enforcement of consent decrees in which state officials agree to do more than federal law requires. Frew v. Hawkins, 540 U.S. 431 (2004). The decree was more detailed than the statute it enforced, but the decree was a permissible means of enforcing federal law, state officials had consented to it, and "once issued, an injunction may be enforced." *Id.* at 440, quoting Hutto v. Finney, 437 U.S. 678, 690 (1978). This part of *Hutto* is discussed in the main volume at 484. If defendants had won, what would be the point of a consent decree with state officials?

Page 493. After note 16, add:

17. The Court relied on the clear statement rule in Raygor v. Regents of University of Minnesota, 534 U.S. 533 (2002), which also illustrates how the effects of immunity can spread out to all sorts of other issues. *Raygor* was an age discrimination claim, filed in federal court under state and federal statutes, alleging supplemental jurisdiction (what used to be called "pendent jurisdiction") over the state-law claims. After the Supreme Court held that states and their instrumentalities are immune from suit under the federal Age Discrimination in Employment Act, plaintiffs dismissed their federal suit and filed the state claims in state court. By now, the state statute of limitations had run, but plaintiffs relied on a tolling provision in the federal supplemental jurisdiction statute. Simplifying just a bit, the statute of limitations on state claims is tolled during the time they were pending in federal court, if they are refiled in state court within 30 days after being dismissed in federal court on grounds going to jurisdiction and not the merits. 28 U.S.C. §1367(d) (2000).

This tolling provision implicated the state's immunity, because waivers of immunity can be subject to conditions, including a limitations period. Some states waive immunity but enact short statutes of limitation especially for claims against the state. *Raygor* involved a general statute of limitations applicable to private defendants as well, but in theory, the legislature might have relied on it when it waived immunity. Plaintiffs thus sought to use the federal tolling provision to expand the state's waiver of immunity. Once that was established, it was obvious that the general language of the federal tolling provision contained no clear statement overriding state sovereign immunity.

18. The tolling provision at issue in *Raygor* was unanimously upheld as applied to suits against a county. Jinks v. Richland County, 538 U.S. 456 (2003). The difference is that immunities derived from the Eleventh Amendment immunity protect only the state and its statewide instrumentalities; local governments are not immune from suit in federal court. The more limited protections available to local governments are explored in the main volume at 1084.

19. The United States tried unsuccessfully to extend *Raygor* in Scarborough v. Principi, 541 U.S. 401 (2004). The Equal Access to Justice Act authorizes awards of attorneys fees against federal agencies and officials, unless the government proves that its position was "substantially justified." The act requires the fee petition to be filed within 30 days of the judgment, and it requires an allegation "that the position of the United States was not substantially justified." Plaintiff successfully claimed disability benefits to which he was entitled as a navy veteran. Eleven days later, he filed his fee petition under the act, but neglected to allege that the position of the United States was not substantially justified. Defendant, the Secretary of Veterans Affairs, moved to dismiss the petition for lack of the required allegation. Plaintiff immediately amended his petition, but by now the 30 days had expired. The Secretary argued that the act was a waiver of immunity, conditioned on all the requirements of the act, and that allowing plaintiff to amend his pleadings would violate the sovereign immunity of the United States.

This was too much for seven justices, who analogized the case to numerous other technical errors that litigants were permitted to fix. The United States had timely notice of the claim and there was no conceivable prejudice. Justices Thomas and Scalia dissented.

2. Suits Against Officers in Their Personal Capacities

Page 503. After note 8.b., add:

A warrant that wholly fails to describe the items to be seized is facially invalid, and the officer who executes such a warrant is not immune. Groh v. Ramirez, 540 U.S. 551 (2004). The application for the warrant, and the affidavit supporting the application, had properly described the items to be seized. The omission in the warrant itself was apparently a clerical error, and the officers confined the search to the terms of the application and affidavit. The officer had typed the warrant himself; at least he is not being sued for the magistrate's clerical error.

Under the clearly-established-law test, the warrant was clearly invalid, and how it came to be invalid was irrelevant. The majority also thought the error was not harmless; the description in the warrant informs the subject of the search of the limits to the search and assures him that the magistrate reviewed those limits. Justice O'Connor crossed over the usual divide to make a majority.

Page 504. After note 8d, add:

A similar issue arose in Wilkie v. Robbins, 2007 WL 1804315 (U.S., June 25, 2007), where plaintiff alleged that government employees had illegally retaliated against him for refusing to convey, without compensation, an easement over his property. There were no cases on government retaliation for exercising rights under the Takings Clause, but there was a settled principle that government cannot retaliate against the exercise of constitutional rights. Justice Ginsburg thought that was enough, at least on the facts: "[I]t is inconceivable that any reasonable official could have believed to be lawful the pernicious harassment Robbins alleges. In the egregious circumstances of this case, the text of the Takings Clause and our retaliation jurisprudence provided the officers fair warning that their behavior impermissibly burdened a constitutional right." Justice Stevens joined in her dissent. The majority did not reach the immunity issue, because it found a different reason for holding that plaintiff had no cause of action. That holding is described in this supplement to page 1038.

Page 504. After note 8.e., add:

f. Hope v. Pelzer, 536 U.S. 730 (2002), reversed a summary judgment in favor of Alabama prison guards who handcuffed plaintiff to a hitching post, outdoors in the summer sun, for two hours on one occasion and seven hours on another. The Eleventh Circuit had held this practice unconstitutional, but also held that there had been no "bright-line rule" making its unconstitutionality obvious in 1995. The Supreme Court reversed, relying on the settled rule that prison authorities may not "unnecessar[ily] and wanton[ly] inflict pain," on a Fifth Circuit holding (binding in the Eleventh because decided before those two circuits were split apart) that it was unconstitutional to handcuff prisoners to a fence for long periods of time, on violations of Alabama's own rules limiting use of the hitching post, and on a Justice Department warning that the hitching post was unconstitutional.

Justice Thomas dissented, partly because he took a different view of the facts, but also because he took a different view of the law. Several unreported district court opinions in Alabama had upheld use of the hitching post; these decisions were more in point than the brief holding in the old Fifth Circuit precedent, which might in any event have been superseded by more recent developments in the law of cruel and unusual punishment. He thought the majority opinion did not come close to showing that the law had been clearly established, and that "qualified immunity jurisprudence had been turned on its head." Justice Scalia and Chief Justice Rehnquist joined the dissent.

Page 504. After note 9, add:

9.1. The Court again announced the requirement of deciding the claim of constitutional right before considering whether the law was clearly settled, matter-of-factly treating this sequence as a settled rule. Chavez v. Martinez, 538 U.S. 760, 766 (2003). The courts of appeals have been surprisingly resistant. Some of them have refused to comply where they find the claim difficult or poorly presented, or where they predict it may arise again in a suit for an injunction; some have feared that any decision might be unappealable dictum. And the resistance has spread to the Supreme Court.

9.2. The problem with appealability reached the Court in dramatic form in Bunting v. Mellen, 541 U.S. 1019 (2004). *Bunting* is just a denial of certiorari, declining to review Mellen v. Bunting, 327 F.3d 355 (4th Cir. 2003). But the debate in separate opinions is highly revealing.

Plaintiffs were cadets at the Virginia Military Institute; defendant Bunting was the superintendent. They sued Bunting in his official capacity for a declaratory judgment that official prayers at supper were unconstitutional and for an injunction prohibiting the prayers; they sued him in his personal capacity for nominal damages. By the time the case got to the court of appeals, plaintiffs had graduated and Bunting had retired. The court held the claims for declaratory and injunctive relief were moot. On the damage claim, it held that the prayers were unconstitutional, but that Bunting had qualified immunity because the law had not been clearly settled. Bunting petitioned for certiorari, and the Court denied the petition. Justice Scalia dissented from the denial of certiorari, prompting Justice Stevens to file a statement in response. The Chief Justice joined Scalia; Justices Ginsburg and Breyer joined Stevens.

Stevens said the Court lacked jurisdiction. The injunctive and declaratory claims were moot, and plaintiffs had not cross-petitioned to challenge the holding that Bunting had qualified immunity. Nothing was left but the dispute over the constitutionality of the prayers. "Whether or not such a dispute would be sufficient to support jurisdiction in different circumstances, it plainly falls short in this case." *Id.* at 1020. Because plaintiffs had graduated and Bunting had retired, there was no live controversy between them over the constitutionality of the prayers. VMI was not a party (presumably because naming it as a party would have violated the Eleventh Amendment). Bunting's successor could have been substituted as the defendant in the official capacity claims for injunction and declaratory judgment, but that would not solve the problem that the plaintiffs had graduated. Stevens also opined that the requirement of deciding the merits before qualified immunity was "an unwise judge-made rule." *Id.*

Justice Scalia thought that the constitutional holding should be reviewable despite the finding of qualified immunity. "That constitutional determination is *not* mere dictum in the ordinary sense, since the whole reason we require it to be set forth . . . is to clarify the law and thus make unavailable repeated claims of qualified immunity in future cases." *Id.* at 1023-24. Either the Court should make such holdings reviewable, or it should not require the merits to be decided before immunity in every case. The Stevens three and the Scalia two would seem to make five votes for sometimes permitting immunity to be decided before the merits, but Scalia said, without explanation, that it was unlikely that such a rule would ever be adopted.

Where does this leave VMI? Justice Stevens noted that there was no injunction to prevent it from reinstituting the prayers. Justice Scalia responded that the precedent of this case would deprive school officials of any qualified immunity defense. If a plaintiff sought real damages, the new Superintendent's only hope to avoid liability would be on pressing the case to the Supreme Court and winning. The risk of any substantial compensatory damages would seem to be small, but the public criticism for seeming to defy the court might be intense.

It is not obvious that qualified immunity should apply to a claim for nominal damages, but several courts have said it does. See Hopkins v. Saunders, 199 F.3d 968, 978 (8th Cir. 1999) (collecting cases). For the dispute over whether a claim for nominal damages is sufficient to avoid mootness, see the supplement to page 250.

9.3. In Brosseau v. Haugen, 543 U.S. 194 (2004), the Supreme Court summarily reversed on qualified immunity without deciding the constitutional issue. A police officer shot a fleeing suspect in the back, fearing that in his desperation to escape he was endangering bystanders. The Ninth Circuit held this shooting to be an unconstitutional seizure of the suspect's person, and held the law on that point clearly settled. The Supreme Court summarily reversed, holding that earlier cases on shooting suspects had not involved claims that it would be dangerous to let the suspect flee. On the priority of the constitutional and immunity issues, the Court said: "We have no occasion in this case to reconsider our instruction . . . that lower courts decide the constitutional question prior to deciding the qualified immunity question. We exercise our summary reversal procedure here simply to correct a clear misapprehension of the qualified immunity standard." Id. at 198 n.3. Is this a case of "Do as I say, not as I do"? The courts of appeals think that they too sometimes have good reasons for inverting the sequence of the questions. Justices Breyer, Scalia, and Ginsburg, concurring, thought the Court should reconsider the issue.

9.4. Pressure on the rule increased in Scott v. Harris, 127 S.Ct. 1769 (2007), another claim that use of deadly force was an unconstitutional seizure. Harris fled a traffic stop at high speed, with officers in hot pursuit. One of the officers eventually tried to end the chase by ramming Harris's car in the rear; Harris lost control of the car and was left quadriplegic. The majority resolved the constitutional issue first, holding that Scott was endangering bystanders and that it was reasonable to try to force him to stop.

(Irrelevant but interesting: This issue turned on a police videotape, inserted into the electronic version of the opinion at www.supremecourtus.gov, which showed, according to the Court, "a Hollywood-style car chase of the most frightening sort." 127 S.Ct. at 1775. Justice Stevens, the oldest Justice by a margin of 13 years, said that if his colleagues had learned to drive before the era of superhighways, when passing on two-lane roads was an essential skill, they wouldn't find the tape so frightening. He accused them of playing jurors.)

Justice Breyer, concurring, said that "commentators, judges, and, in this case, 28 States in an *amicus* brief," had urged the Court to reconsider the requirement that the constitutional issue be resolved before the immunity issue. He would not reverse the priority of the two issues; he would let courts resolve them in either order depending on what made sense in each case. The Court declined the invitation on the ground that here, the constitutional issue was easy, so it made sense to resolve it first whether or not it was required.

Justice Breyer repeated this argument in Morse v. Frederick, 2007 WL 1804317 (U.S., June 25, 2007), where a high school principal suspended a student who displayed (and refused to take down) a 14-foot banner that said "Bong Hits 4 Jesus." The majority held that the banner was not constitutionally protected speech; three dissenters thought it was protected. Justice Breyer thought the free speech issue was difficult and the immunity issue easy; he voted for the principal on the ground of qualified immunity.

9.5. In Los Angeles County v. Rettele, 127 S.Ct. 1989 (2007), the Court summarily reversed a holding that police had unreasonably executed a search warrant by rousting a nude couple out of bed and forcing them to remain nude and standing for several minutes while the police confirmed that no one else was in the apartment and no weapons were within reach. The police had the wrong apartment. Justice Stevens and Ginsburg, concurring, would have decided the case on qualified immunity grounds and would have repudiated "the unwise practice of deciding constitutional questions in advance of the necessity for doing so." *Id.* at 1994 (Stevens, J., concurring). This would seem to go well beyond Justice Breyer's position, and to insist on deciding the immunity issue first. That would leave the original problem, that in contexts where possibly illegal conduct could not be anticipated and enjoined, issues not clearly settled might never become clearly settled.

9.6. In Wilkie v. Robbins, 2007 WL 1804315 (U.S., June 25, 2007), the entire Court addressed a difficult merits issue in a case up on interlocutory appeal based on denial of qualified immunity. No one appears to have suggested taking up immunity first, and no one explained why not. Maybe the explanation is that defendants would have lost on immunity, but they won on the ground that there is no cause of action for damages for the constitutional violation plaintiff alleged. The immunity issue is further described in this supplement to page 504; the cause-of-action issue is described in this supplement to page 1038.

Page 505. After note 12, add:

But the doctrine does not permit federal employees to immediately appeal an order rejecting their motion to dismiss a *Bivens* claim (a suit against federal employees for violating the Constitution) on the ground that a court had already rejected a claim against the United States under the Federal Tort Claims Act and based on the same underlying facts. The Court held that that defense, created by 28 U.S.C. §2676 (2000), is more like claim preclusion than immunity, and does not justify the special protections of the collateral order doctrine. Will v. Hallock, 546 U.S. 345 (2006). *Bivens* appears in the main volume and supplement at 1033.

Page 507. After note 5, add:

5.1. The Court has applied *Ryder* to invalidate a decision of a court of appeals panel with two judges authorized to sit and one not so authorized. Khanh Phuong Nguyen v. United States, 539 U.S. 69 (2003). The third judge on the panel was a judge of the United States District Court for the District of the Northern Mariana Islands, who was not appointed under Article III of the Constitution and does not have life tenure. The Court rejected arguments that there had been a quorum of validly appointed judges, and that petitioner had not complained of the defect when there was time to fix it.

CHAPTER FIVE

PREVENTING HARM WITHOUT COERCION: DECLARATORY REMEDIES

A. DECLARATORY JUDGMENTS

Page 525. After note 8, add:

8.1. Medimmune, Inc. v. Genentech, Inc., 127 S.Ct. 764 (2007), rejected a substantial challenge to the use of declaratory judgments in private disputes. Genentech claims that one of its patents covers Medimmune's principal product. Medimmune is a much smaller company; it decided that it could not afford the risk of being enjoined or of incurring liability for treble damages and attorneys' fees. So it entered into a licensing agreement with Genentech, promising to pay royalties until or unless the patent was held invalid, and stating that it was doing so under protest and reserving all its rights. It has paid the royalties due under the agreement. Then it sued for a declaratory judgment that the Genentech patent is invalid.

The Federal Circuit held that there was no case or controversy! 427 F.3d 958 (Fed. Cir. 2005). Medimmune faced no risk of suit, because it was in full compliance with the licensing agreement. In effect, the court says that a litigant seeking to use a declaratory judgment to resolve its *Young* dilemma must leave itself exposed to the risk of liability in order to preserve its standing to file the declaratory judgment claim.

Justice Scalia, writing for the Court, took it as settled that a citizen facing a coercive threat from the government need not expose himself to the threat in order to create a case or controversy. He saw no reason why that rule should not also apply to coercive threats from other private entities, and found the *Altvater* case (discussed in *Cardinal Chemical* at 519) to have decided the issue.

Justice Thomas dissented. He thought that Steffel v. Thompson (in the main volume at 531), was limited to government coercion, and perhaps to the threat of prosecution and imprisonment. He thought that Medimmune was simply seeking an advisory opinion about a hypothetical dispute that would arise if it quit paying royalties. But the other way to characterize those same facts is that there was an actual (and rancorous) controversy about the validity of the patent, and an immediate and concrete choice of action depended on the resolution of that controversy: If Medimmune prevailed on the validity issue, it would stop paying royalties.

Justice Thomas apparently thought that *Altvater* and *Cardinal Chemical* were limited to cases where there was a suit for patent and infringement and then a counterclaim for a declaratory judgment that the patent was invalid. Of course that is not what *Cardinal Chemical* said; see the main volume at 520. It is hard to know how far Justice Thomas would have carried his position, but it would surely have led to a substantial contraction in the use of declaratory judgments between private parties.

8.2. A patent scholar reports that the Federal Circuit continues to resist the Declaratory Judgment Act in patent cases and the view of that Act expressed in cases like *Cardinal Chemical*. Lorelei Ritchie de Larena, *Re-evaluating Declaratory Judgment Jurisdiction in Intellectual Property Disputes*, 83 Ind. L.J. ---- (2007 (forthcoming), available at *http://ssrn.com/abstract=967336*. The Federal Circuit's application of the Declaratory Judgment Act continues to be stingy, and Professor de Larena believes that a patent holder who avoids explicitly threatening to sue still has substantial power to deter competitors without risking a lawsuit. Similar language appears in many copyright and trademark declaratory judgment cases, but the declaratory judgment action is much more likely to be permitted. The difference is that appeals in copyright and trademark cases go to the geographic circuits, but every patent appeal goes to the Federal Circuit.

Page 528. After note 3, add:

3.1. There is an application of these rules in Holmes Group v. Vornado Air Circulation Systems, Inc., 535 U.S. 826 (2002). Plaintiff sued for a declaratory judgment that its product did not violate defendant's trade dress (a form of trademark claim based on the distinctive appearance of the product and its packaging), and an injunction restraining defendant from accusing plaintiff of trade-dress infringement in its promotional materials. Defendant counterclaimed for patent infringement; this was a compulsory counterclaim, meaning that it was so factually linked to the trade-dress claims that it would be barred if not asserted.

The Court had no difficulty concluding that the case did not arise under the patent laws, because the well-pleaded complaint rule looks only to plaintiff's claims, not defendant's. Nothing in the opinion suggests that the case did not arise under federal law, but here it mattered that it arose under the trademark laws and not under the patent laws. Because it did not arise under the patent laws, the appeal went to the appropriate geographic circuit and not to the Federal Circuit. This rule raises an obvious potential for appellate forum shopping in disputes with more than one kind of intellectual property claim.

Page 537. After the first paragraph of note 3, add:

Broad summaries of detailed doctrines make it easy to err, and I succumbed. *Younger* has not been extended to "most civil proceedings." I think it would be more accurate to say that it has been extended to most civil proceedings to which a state agency or official is a party, and to enforcement of state judgments even between private parties. Parallel state and federal litigation in ordinary civil cases is fairly common, and while one court often stays its proceedings in deference to the other, that is not required or universal. The leading case permitting both actions to proceed simultaneously still appears to be Kline v. Burke Construction Co., 260 U.S. 226 (1922). I focused on this distinction, and noticed the overgeneralization in the main volume, in the course of summarizing Exxon Mobil Corp. v. Saudi Basic Industries Corp., in this supplement to page 546.

Page 546. After note 10, add:

The en banc D.C. Circuit has assumed that *Mancuso* is still good law. Clarke v. United States, 915 F.2d 699, 702 (D.C. Cir. 1990). *Clarke* involved not a preliminary injunction, but a final declaratory judgment that the law was unconstitutional, affirmed on appeal, with a petition for rehearing denied on the merits, but set for argument to consider whether the case had become moot. The government sought to have the declaratory judgment vacated as moot, because the law at issue was an appropriations rider that had been allowed to lapse, and it conceded that it could not prosecute for violations committed under the protection of the declaratory judgment. The court also said that federal judicial power to prevent federal prosecutions presents a much clearer and simpler question than *MITE*, which involved federal judicial power to prevent state prosecutions.

NOTES ON FEDERAL LITIGATION AFTER STATE-COURT JUDGMENTS

1. The usual rules for protecting finality of judgments and preventing repeated litigation of the same issues are the rules of claim preclusion and issue preclusion (still occasionally known as res judicata and collateral estoppel), which are part of the first-year Civil Procedure course. But occasionally the Supreme Court has addressed these issues with variations on Younger v. Harris. In Huffman v. Pursue, Ltd., 420 U.S. 592 (1975), the Court held that *Younger* barred a suit to enjoin enforcement of a state-court injunction, at least until state appeals had been exhausted. It is not clear why issue preclusion was not a more straightforward ground for decision, and it is almost unimaginable that the Court would entertain such a suit *after* state appeals had been exhausted. Interjurisdictional claim and issue preclusion is codified in the Full Faith and Credit Act, 28 U.S.C. §1738 (2000), which requires that state judgments be given "the same full faith and credit in every court within the United States . . . as they have by law or usage in the courts of such State . . . from which they are taken."

2. Another variation is the *Rooker-Feldman* doctrine, derived from Rooker v. Fidelity Trust Co., 263 U.S. 413 (1923), and District of Columbia Court of Appeals v. Feldman, 460 U.S. 462 (1983). *Rooker-Feldman* bars a federal trial court from reviewing a state-court judgment, and lower courts had broadly construed it to apply to a variety of claims that might in anyway be construed as interfering with a state-court judgment. The Supreme Court unanimously confined the doctrine to its original facts in Exxon

Mobil Corp. v. Saudi Basic Industries Corp., 544 U.S. 280 (2005). *Rooker-Feldman* now applies only to "cases brought by state-court losers complaining of injuries caused by state-court judgments rendered before the district court proceedings commenced and inviting district court review and rejection of those judgments. *Rooker-Feldman* does not otherwise override or supplant preclusion doctrine or augment the circumscribed doctrines that allow federal courts to stay or dismiss proceedings in deference to state-court actions." *Id.* at 281. Except in the unusual context of a state-court loser filing a new federal claim directed squarely at setting aside the judgment, this should mean that litigators have one fewer federal abstention doctrine to worry about.

The Court viewed *Exxon Mobil* as a legitimate example of dual litigation. Saudi Basic sued Exxon Mobil in state court; Exxon Mobil counterclaimed. Exxon Mobil also filed its claim in a separate action in federal court "to protect itself in the event it lost in state court on grounds (such as the state statute of limitations) that might not preclude relief in the federal venue." When Exxon Mobil eventually got a judgment on its counterclaim in the state trial court, the federal court dismissed its federal action on *Rooker-Feldman* grounds, even though state appeals were pending. The Supreme Court reversed: Exxon Mobil filed its federal claim before the judgment in state court, and Exxon Mobil had not lost in state court; under the new formulation of the rule, either of these grounds is enough.

3. The Court re-emphasized *Exxon Mobil* in Lance v. Dennis, 546 U.S. 459 (2006), holding that *Rooker-Feldman* does *not* apply to parties in privity with state court losers. The lower courts had held citizens of Colorado barred by an earlier state-court judgment against Colorado's General Assembly and Secretary of State. That may be the right result under the Colorado law of issue preclusion, but that is irrelevant to *Rooker-Feldman*. The Court explained that the Full Faith and Credit Act incorporates the state law of preclusion, and that state law should not be preempted by a uniform federal law of preclusion developed under *Rooker-Feldman*. *Rooker-Feldman* is a very narrow doctrine designed to prevent losing litigants from, in effect, appealing state court judgments to federal district courts.

B. QUIET TITLE AND THE LIKE

Page 554. After note 11, add:

12. A former property owner used quiet title to challenge the legality of a federal tax sale, alleging that it had not received the notice required by statute and suing the company that bought the property at the sale. Grable & Sons Metal Products, Inc. v. Darue Engineering & Manufacturing, 545 U.S. 308 (2005). No one disputed that quiet title was an appropriate remedy, but on the merits, the plaintiff lost. The Court did not treat quiet title merely as a remedy (which it is), but as a state-law cause of action (which it also is).

D. DECLARATORY RELIEF AT LAW

1. Nominal Damages

Page 562. At the end of the note on Nominal Damages, add:

The Ninth Circuit has held that when nominal damages are awarded in a class action, the award must run to each class member. Cummings v. Connell, 402 F.3d 936 (9th Cir. 2005). The difference is significant; the court awarded $1.00 to each of 37,000 class members. The district court had considered awarding one cent to each class member; it rejected that alternative on the grounds that it "would more trivialize plaintiffs' constitutional rights than vindicate them," and that defendant would still bear the cost of cutting 37,000 checks. Instead, it awarded $1.00 each to the seven class representatives. Cases elsewhere, collected in the Ninth Circuit opinion, appear to be split.

The district court also awarded substantial attorneys' fees in *Cummings*. The Ninth Circuit appeared to approve, but it remanded the fee issue so the district court could consider whether a judgment for $37,000 instead of $7.00 justified a larger fee.

CHAPTER SIX

BENEFIT TO DEFENDANT AS THE
MEASURE OF RELIEF: RESTITUTION

A. DISGORGING PROFITS

1. The Basic Principle

Page 579. After note 6, add:

7. The new *Restatement* project has at last reached restitution of profits from wrongdoing. *Restatement (Third) of Restitution and Unjust Enrichment* §§40-44 (Tent. Draft 4, 2005). These sections provide for disgorgement of profits acquired by intentional tortious conduct. Sections 40-43 address trespass and conversion, misappropriation of financial assets, interference with intellectual property and similar rights, and breach of fiduciary or confidential relations. Section 44, entitled "Interference with Other Protected Interests," is a catchall. Section 44(1) provides: "In a case not covered by the rules of §§40-43, a person who obtains a benefit by conscious interference with another's legally protected interests is accountable to the other for the benefit so obtained, unless competing legal objectives make such liability inappropriate." Section 44(3) gives some intelligible content to the unless clause.

The distinction between conscious wrongdoing and mere negligence or innocent mistake is explicit throughout. The details of the sections vary, because "conscious wrongdoing" is not a bright line category; different legal and factual contexts generate different kinds of questions about culpability and measurement of profits, and different balances of competing interests relevant to answering those questions. This draft has now been tentatively approved by the Council and Membership of the American Law Institute.

The question whether claims under these sections are substantive claims in unjust enrichment or remedies for the underlying torts is briefly addressed in the "Reporter's Note to Introductory Note" at page 45 of Tent. Draft 4. The Reporter concludes that the choice of explanations presents a "purely academic" question, except as it relates to statutes of limitations, where it becomes "intensely practical."

Page 603. After note 10, add:

Professor Kull and the American Law Institute have undertaken, with substantial success, to state a rule and make sense of this whole area. *Restatement (Third) of Restitution and Unjust Enrichment* §39 (Tent. Draft 4, 2005). The section authorizes disgorgement of profits from breaches that are both "material and opportunistic." A breach is opportunistic if it satisfies three requirements. The breach must be "deliberate." The breach must be "profitable" in the sense that defendant earns more by breaching and paying damages than by performing. And third, damages must be "inadequate," with the additional guidance that "damages are ordinarily an adequate remedy if they can be used to acquire a full equivalent to the promised performance in a substitute transaction," and are ordinarily inadequate if they cannot be so used. The proposed rule makes sense of 16 illustrations in the comments, each based on a real case.

B. RESTITUTION AND CONTRACT

1. The Basics

Page 626. After note 9.b, add:

The right to rescission for substantial breach is newly restated in *Restatement (Third) of Restitution and Unjust Enrichment* §37 (Tent. Draft 3, 2004). The draft uses the unfortunate phrase "total breach," inherited from the *Restatement (Second) of Contracts*. But the comments emphasize that "total breach" does not mean that defendant did absolutely nothing toward performance of his contract. Rather, in both restatements that use the phrase, "total breach" means a breach that justifies the other party in stopping her own performance and treating the contract as at an end.

2. New Frontiers, or Dead Ends?

Page 644. Before note 1, add:

0.1. On remand, the trial court awarded the $380 million in reliance damages. Glendale also claimed its net losses on Broward as additional reliance damages, but in calculating those losses, it treated its assumption of Broward's liabilities as an investment in Broward. The trial court rejected that claim as inconsistent with the Federal Circuit's holding that the assumption of Broward's liabilities was too speculative to serve as a basis for recovery. Glendale Federal Bank FSB v. United States, 54 Fed. Cl. 8 (Ct. Fed. Claims 2002), *aff'd*, 378 F.3d 1308 (Fed. Cir. 2004).

Page 652. After note 12, add:

13. My former colleague Mark Gergen has offered a serious alternate explanation for cases like *Boomer*. Mark P. Gergen, *Restitution as a Bridge over Troubled Contractual Waters*, 71 Fordham L. Rev. 709 (2002). Distinguish two plausible explanations for the huge cost overrun in *Boomer*. One, plaintiff misbid the job, either because of some mistake that could have been avoided, or because of some unpredictable difficulty in performance, like hard rock where he expected dirt. And two, delayed or improper or inadequate performance by defendant drove the cost up. Suppose Boomer had a huge cost overrun because Muir did not deliver promised equipment and supplies on time, or did not get other subcontractors out of the way when he was supposed to.

In a case where the first set of explanations applies, plaintiff made a disastrous contract and is rescued by defendant's breach. Under the second set of explanations, defendant's breach caused the disaster. A *Boomer*-style remedy in the first set of cases is a windfall to plaintiff, or at least a lucky break, even if you approve of the result. But a *Boomer*-style remedy in the second set may be rough justice; it puts the burden of the cost-overrun on the party who caused it. Gergen reports that a majority of cases like *Boomer* are in this second category.

In this second set of cases, plaintiff has a straightforward damage remedy for the contract price plus the additional expense caused by defendant's breach. But that would require proof of causation, which may be complex or difficult. And there may be limitation of remedy clauses (no damage for delay is a common clause in construction contracts) that preclude such a damage claim. The restitution claim avoids those difficulties. The contract is rescinded, so limitation of remedies clauses are no longer in effect, and the work is revalued free of the contract, so causation doesn't matter and no one has to prove damages. But avoiding the difficulties means that the restitution theory is available even when defendant did not cause the cost overrun, or when the court in a damage action would have upheld the limitation of remedy clause. The restitution theory may do rough justice in a range of cases, but it is seriously overinclusive.

Another way to simplify proof of causation is with presumptions. If plaintiff proves that defendant's breach was extensive and caused much expense in proportion to the scope of the work, some courts will presume that the entire cost overrun is attributable to defendant. This is a damage theory, and it seems to me to provide a much better allocation of risk than the restitution theory in *Boomer*. *Boomer* plaintiffs have to prove material breach, but nothing about causation of the cost overrun.

14. The new *Restatement* squarely rejects *Boomer*, subjecting restitution of the value of the partly finished work to a limit equal to the value of that work as determined by the contract. *Restatement (Third) of Restitution and Unjust Enrichment* §38 (Tent. Draft 3, 2004). Comment d to this section endorses the claim for damages when defendant's breach caused the cost overrun, and urges courts not to restrict that remedy with excessive evidentiary requirements.

C. TRACING DEFENDANT'S BENEFIT: RESTITUTION AND INSOLVENCY

Page 687. After note 3, add:

3.1. The Massachusetts court recently decided a case where the divorced couple's agreement required the wife to maintain $200,000 in life insurance for the benefit of the children, but mentioned no specific policy. Foster v. Hurley, 826 N.E.2d 719 (Mass. 2005). She had a $100,000 policy through her employer at the time of the divorce in 1995, and that policy had increased in value (probably it was tied to a multiple of her salary) to $168,000 by the time of her death. She had another policy, acquired after the divorce when she took a second job, for $31,000.

The four-judge majority held that the first husband, as trustee for the children, was entitled to be "equitably substitut[ed]" as the beneficiary of the policy in effect at the time of the agreement. He got the whole $168,000, not just the value that policy had had in 1995. So the identity of the policy mattered, but the amount did not. The first husband could not reach the second policy, acquired later; there was no explicit or implicit promise about that policy. The wife's wrong consisted of failing to acquire another policy for the benefit of the children, but that wrong could not be linked to the after-acquired policy for the benefit of the second husband. The coincidence of amounts -- $32,000 needed for the children, $31,000 acquired for the second husband -- was irrelevant.

Three dissenters would have given the first husband both policies. And in comments that speak to all the variations on these cases, the dissenters said:

> If she had given the defendant anything but the "encumbered" proceeds of an insurance policy -- say an automobile, stock certificates, cash, or even proceeds of an insurance policy to the extent the amount of proceeds exceeded the $200,000 obligation in the separation agreement -- equitable substitution would be unavailable. But, by choosing the precise form of asset covered by the separation agreement -- insurance policy proceeds -- when the deceased had not first satisfied her life insurance obligation under the separation agreement, her intent to avoid the obligation coupled with the specific asset selected combine to bring the policy within the well-established authority of a court acting in equity to protect children from the connivances of a divorced parent.

Id. at 730 (Greaney, J., dissenting). So in Justice Greaney's view, it has to be an insurance policy, but it need not be the same insurance policy, a policy mentioned by the parties, or a policy in existence at the time the obligation arose. Does that ascribe magic significance to the nature of the asset? Or is it just another crude but defensible compromise between competing claims?

Page 689. After note 1, add:

1.1. A spectacular public example of an attempted fraudulent transfer arose in the litigation alleging securities fraud and improper insurance practices by the giant insurer, American International Group. Maurice Greenberg, the founder and chairman of the company, gave 41.4 million AIG shares, worth $2.6 billion at the time, to his wife without consideration. He made the gift on March 11, 2005, after the company had been sued but before he personally had been sued. The gift could not be hidden; he duly reported this large transfer of shares in a required filing with the Securities and Exchange Commission.

It is hard to imagine how he thought he would get away with this, or why it even seemed worth trying. He is said to own the equivalent of another 120 million shares through a holding company, and he has said the gift was "completely misunderstood," so perhaps he thought that ample assets remained available to his creditors and that the gift was for some legitimate reason, such as estate planning. Three Ohio public pension plans moved to rescind the gift as a fraudulent transfer and to appoint a receiver to hold the shares until the end of the case. Gretchen Morgenson, *Plaintiff Asks Court to Rescind Greenberg's Transfer of A.I.G. Stock to Wife*, N.Y. Times C6 (May 27, 2005). A month later, Greenberg and his wife reversed the gift and put the issue to rest. Jenny Anderson, *A.I.G. Posts 44% Earnings Rise Under New Leader*, N.Y. Times C2 (June 29, 2005).

Page 696. After note 5, add:

5.1. The court refused restitution on highly similar facts in Jacoby v. Jacoby, 100 P.3d 852 (Wyo. 2004). In *Jacoby*, the older couple refinanced their property to raise money to build the house, and the younger couple agreed to make payments to them. When the dust settled after the younger couple's divorce, the older couple was living in the new house, their old house was rented, and they had an additional $50,000 in mortgage liens on their property.

The state supreme court reversed an equitable lien in favor of the younger wife:

> While it is true that the value of appellants' real property has been enhanced, those facts alone do not make the appellants "unjustly enriched." An extended mortgage late in life is not "enrichment." . . . [The equitable lien] ignores the realities facing this older couple. Instead of having their son's family next door, and instead of receiving half of the increased monthly mortgage payments, the appellants now share their property with renters, and they pay more than twice what they used to pay as a monthly mortgage payment. Their additional reward, from this lawsuit, is a $64,600 lien on their property. This is simply wrong. "Let no good deed go unpunished" is not an equitable maxim.

Id. at 857. Two dissenters (on a five-judge court) relied on *Robinson*. The majority suggested that if the project had failed because the *older* couple divorced, "the opposite conclusion -- that they had been unjustly enriched -- might readily be true." *Id.* at 857 n.3.

We do not have the trial court's opinion, but it is hard to see how the younger wife's share of the house could be worth $64,000 if the older couple was given proper credit for the mortgage. The trial-court judgment does not appear to be based on appreciation, because we are told that he rejected a constructive trust claim as excessive. The choice between equitable lien and constructive trust is taken up in the notes that follow in the main volume.

Page 699. After note 12, add:

13. The Supreme Court recently relied on old cases, from before the merger of law and equity, allowing parties to create an equitable lien by agreement. Sereboff v. Mid Atlantic Medical Services, Inc.,

126 S.Ct. 1869 (2006). Sereboff's employer-sponsored medical insurance policy provided that if he collected benefits for the treatment of injuries caused by a third party, he would reimburse the insurer for those benefits from "all recoveries from a third party (whether by lawsuit, settlement, or otherwise)." Sereboff was injured and collected $750,000 from the tortfeasor, but refused to reimburse $75,000 in medical expenses paid by her insurer.

The medical insurer's claim could not be a simple suit for contract damages, because ERISA (the Employee Retirement and Income Security Act, 29 U.S.C. §1132(a) (2000)), allows only "appropriate equitable relief," not legal relief. For this aspect of the dispute, see the main volume and supplement and 1115-1117. The Court held that the insurance policy created an equitable lien, and that the insurer could enforce this equitable lien at least against funds specifically derived from the tort settlement. But this was a two-party dispute between insurer and insured; surely it should not be read as holding that this equitable lien would be good against other creditors of the insured in the absence of any kind of filing or notice.

E. REPLEVIN, EJECTMENT, AND THE LIKE

Page 716. After note 4, add:

4.1. A somewhat similar case, with a harsher result and a simpler legal theory, is Menzel v. List, 246 N.E.2d 742 (N.Y. 1969). Plaintiffs (the Menzels) bought a Marc Chagall painting in 1932, in Belgium, for about $150. They fled Belgium when the Nazis invaded, and the painting disappeared until it turned up in a Paris art gallery in 1955. A New York gallery bought it for $2,800, and resold it to List for $4,000. List allowed an image to be printed in an art book, with credit to his collection, and the Menzels found their painting in the art book in 1962. They sued List in replevin; the jury awarded the painting to the Menzels, and in the alternative, valued the painting at $22,500. List returned the painting to the Menzels.

Meanwhile, List had impleaded the New York gallery, alleging breach of the warranty of title. The gallery argued that the measure of damages was the $4,000 purchase price plus interest; the court awarded $22,500, the value at the time of trial. The court focused on the general principle of putting plaintiffs in as good a position as if the contract had been performed; it made no mention of more specific rules about valuing the goods as of the time and place of delivery (in contract) or the misappropriation (in tort). It reasoned that awarding $4,000 plus interest would restore List only to as good a position as if the contract had never been made. So the court awarded List his expectancy, but expectancy calculated as of seven years after the contract. It reported that cases around the country were in disarray.

4.2. The New York court cited *Menzel* in In re Estate of Rothko, 372 N.E.2d 291 (1977), a famous case on breach of trust. The principal assets in Mark Rothko's estate were 798 of his paintings; his executors sold them for less than fair market value in a rushed transaction tainted by conflict of interest. But *Rothko* relied principally on a more settled body of trust law. A trustee who is authorized to sell trust assets and honestly sells at too low a price is liable only for the value at the time of sale. A trustee who is not authorized to sell at all, and sells anyway, is liable for the value at the time of trial if that is greater; the court called this "appreciation damages." Viewing the serious conflict of interest in *Rothko* as wrongdoing more analogous to the case of trustees not authorized to sell at all, it awarded appreciation damages. This is a variation on the statement in *Welch* that "the conscious wrongdoer cannot make a profit and is responsible for losses." For the conscious wrongdoer, the court measured losses in the most generous way.

4.3. Jennifer Neelon, a law student at the University of Idaho with an interest in antique silver, undertook to learn more about *Welch*. She reports that a castor originally meant a salt or pepper shaker, and eventually came to include other small containers for condiments. More remarkably, it appears that at the time of the litigation, defendant and one of the plaintiffs were both members of the Harvard faculty.

CHAPTER SEVEN

PUNITIVE REMEDIES

A. PUNITIVE DAMAGES

1. Common Law and Statutes

Page 729. After note 6, add:

6.1. For a detailed review of *Grimshaw* and the Pinto, see Gary T. Schwartz, *The Myth of the Ford Pinto Case*, 43 Rutgers L. Rev. 1013 (1991). Professor Schwartz reviewed the trial transcript and interviewed the lead lawyers for both sides. He also examined facts and data developed in Ford's criminal trial in Indiana on a charge of reckless homicide, where the jury acquitted, and in federal regulatory proceedings. He concludes that overall, the Pinto was no more dangerous than other small cars. It had a much higher rate of fires in rear end collisions, but probably not uniquely so, and even for the Pinto, such fires occurred in a tiny percentage of all accidents. The government found 27 deaths and 24 injuries in rear-end collisions with Pintos from 1971 to 1977; an unknown fraction of these involved high speed collisions where no available technology could have kept the gas tank intact.

At pages 1020-1026, Schwartz gives careful attention to the chart reproduced in note 5. This chart was part of the regulatory proceeding, was not admitted in evidence in the *Grimshaw* trial, and was not about Pintos or rear-end collisions. Schwartz concludes that it was a cost-benefit assessment of gas-tank fires in rollovers for all cars produced in the United States in a year. But he also concludes that a "limited core of the Pinto story remains." Some of the technology suggested by plaintiffs was still experimental when the Pinto was designed, and some of plaintiffs proposals were simply unworkable, but four changes with a combined cost of $9 per car "clearly would have improved the Pinto's safety to some appreciable extent." "It is plausible to believe, then, that because of these costs, Ford decided not to improve the Pinto's design, knowing that its decision would increase the chances of the loss of consumer life." *Id.* at 1034-1035.

Page 730. After note 7, add:

7.1. A series of studies with mock jurors is reported in Cass R. Sunstein, Reid Hastie, John W. Payne, David A Schkade, & W. Kip Viscusi, *Punitive Damages: How Juries Decide* (University of Chicago Press 2002). Samples of citizens eligible for jury duty were assembled in five states. Experimenters presented case summaries, generally based on real cases, and systematically varied the presentation to test various hypotheses. Together the studies included more than 8,000 potential jurors and more than 600 mock juries; the same or similar cases were also presented to several hundred sitting judges.

These studies have been widely and severely criticized on methodological grounds. The case summaries were extremely short, sometimes as short as six sentences, and the summaries were tilted heavily in favor of plaintiffs; the task set for potential jurors bore little or no resemblance to a real trial. Exxon paid for the research. Neil Vidmar, *Experimental Simulations and Tort Reform: Avoidance, Error, and Overreaching in Sunstein et al.'s Punitive Damages*, 53 Emory L.J. 1359 (2004) (elaborating these and other criticisms and collecting other negative reviews). I thus introduce some of the Sunstein findings here with considerable caution; they are at most suggestive.

The studies support the hypothesis that juries punish explicit cost-benefit analysis. More surprisingly, defendants that used a higher value for human life in their cost-benefit studies were punished more, even though using a higher value for human life is more protective of human life and leads to taking more safety precautions. The authors speculate that mention of the higher number may lead jurors to think in terms of larger numbers when they assess punitives.

In one of the studies, juries were told the chances that a person doing what defendant had done would be detected and get sued, and these chances were varied twenty-fold. There was no effect on the resulting punitive damage verdicts. Some juries were given an instruction on optimal deterrence, but most of these juries were unable or unwilling to follow that instruction.

There were powerful hindsight effects. In one experiment, potential jurors were given a description of a known risk on a railroad track. Two-thirds said the railroad should be excused from fixing the problem. Other potential jurors were given an identical description of the risk, with the extra fact that a serious accident had resulted; two-thirds of these jurors thought the railroad had been reckless and that punitive damages should be assessed.

Judges generally exhibited the same biases as potential jurors, but to a lesser degree. They did considerably better at controlling their hindsight bias; in the railroad problem, 15% would have required the railroad to fix the problem before the accident, and only 23% would have imposed punitive damages after learning of the accident.

Page 731. At the end of note 8, add:

The Supreme Court seems to be experimenting with a different approach to this problem, narrowing the scope of similar misconduct that can be shown to each jury. See State Farm Mutual Automobile Insurance Co. v. Campbell, 538 U.S. 408 (2003), excerpted in the supplement to page 741.

Page 731. At the end of the first paragraph of note 9, add:

9.1. *Engle* has been reversed on multiple grounds -- that punitives could not be determined for the class before liability had been determined to the class, and that the verdict was grossly excessive because it would bankrupt the defendants. But the jury findings about defendants' intentional wrongdoing would be binding in individual actions by class members, who would have to prove only those facts specific to individual claimants. Engle v. Liggett Group Inc., 945 So.2d 1246 (Fla. 2006), *cert. filed*, 75 U.S.L.W. 3669 (May 21, 2007, No. 06-1545). The tobacco industry filed the cert petition, arguing that the jury findings are too ambiguous to be binding in individual actions and that the entire case is preempted by federal tobacco regulation.

9.2. The West Virginia court has considered whether to squeeze a little more into the class part of the case. In re Tobacco Litigation, 624 S.E.2d 738 (W. Va. 2005). The trial court has 1,100 consolidated tobacco cases. It proposed a mass trial of liability, including whether punitive damages should be awarded and determination of a multiplier for assessing punitive damages. Then there will be individual trials on compensatory damages and any other individual issues, and the pre-determined multiplier will be applied to each compensatory award to determine that individual plaintiff's punitives. Responding to a certified question, the Supreme Court of Appeals held only that this plan does not violate *State Farm v. Campbell*, excerpted at this supplement to page 741; it did not consider any other possible objections.

9.3. On remand in *Exxon*, the district court entered a remittitur to $4 billion, defended the jury's award of $5 billion, and clearly indicated his disagreement with the court of appeals. 236 F. Supp. 2d 1043 (D. Alaska 2002). In an unreported order, the Ninth Circuit vacated and remanded for reconsideration in light of State Farm v. Campbell. The trial court vacated its $4-billion judgment. 296 F. Supp. 2d 1071 (D. Alaska 2004). It concluded that $5 billion was justified under *State Farm*, because defendant's conduct had been highly reprehensible, punitives were less than ten times compensatories ($513 million), and civil and criminal penalties could have exceed $5 billion. But the court of appeals had instructed him to reduce the amount, so he would -- to $4.5 billion. Note that this is an increase from the $4 billion that had been vacated.

The court of appeals again vacated the judgment, and this time remanded for entry of judgment in the amount of $2.5 billion, emphasizing that the litigation should now end. In re the Exxon Valdez, 2007 WL 1490455 at *30 (9th Cir., May 23, 2007). Exxon's conduct in knowingly letting a relapsed alcoholic command a supertanker loaded with oil was "in the higher realm of reprehensibility, but not in the highest realm." *Id.* at *23. It was reckless, not intentional. Ratios near the upper end of single digits were generally reserved "for the most egregious forms of intentional misconduct, such as threats of violence and intentional racial discrimination." *Id.* at *28. The reprehensibility of Exxon's conduct was substantially mitigated by its response to the accident, engaging in vigorous clean up efforts, setting up a claims process, and voluntarily paying $493 million in compensation without being sued.

Exxon argued that the $493 million it had paid voluntarily were not compensatory damages at all, and the ratio of punitives to compensatories should be based only on the $20 million actually awarded in judgments. The court rejected that argument; acceptance of responsibility was mitigating, not exonerating. "No criminal defendant guilty of a serious wrong ordinarily resulting in lengthy imprisonment could reasonably assume that he would receive no imprisonment at all if he promptly pleaded guilty." *Id.* at *25. So the total damages were $513 million (rounded to $500 million), the appropriate ratio was in the mid-single digits, or 5:1, and the appropriate punitive damage award was $2.5 billion.

Judge Browning, dissenting on the panel, would have found the wrongdoing intentional and mitigation irrelevant; he would have approved a 9:1 ratio and affirmed the $4.5 billion award. Judge Bea, dissenting from denial of rehearing en banc, thought that $513 million in compensatories was so substantial that a ratio of 1:1 was probably more appropriate -- an idea that appears briefly in State Farm v. Campbell, excerpted at supplement to page 741.

Judge Kozinski, joined by Judge Bea, dissented from denial of rehearing en banc on a more fundamental ground. An early Supreme Court decision held that punitive damages cannot be awarded against ship owners in admiralty "based solely on the fault of captain and crew." *Id.* at *1, citing The Amiable Nancy, 16 U.S. 546 (1818). According to Judge Kozinski, other circuits adhere to this precedent but the Ninth Circuit has repudiated it. But that principle appears to be irrelevant to the holding in *Exxon*. The court did not award punitive damages based on the fault of the captain and crew. It awarded punitive damages based on a decision made on land, at higher levels of the organization chart, to allow a relapsed alcoholic to captain a supertanker in dangerous waters. It is reasonable to expect a cert petition raising at least the two issues in the dissents from denial of rehearing en banc, and perhaps other issues as well.

Page 733. After note 6, add:

6.1. All this attention to jury instructions may have little effect on juries. The studies by Sunstein *et al.* found that juries were generally unable to follow instructions and spent little time discussing them, although the allocation of time might have been distorted by the sharply compressed time allowed for deliberations in the studies. The more time a mock jury did spend discussing instructions, the less likely it was to award punitives and the smaller the likely amount. Most striking, the researchers asked some jurors who had completed their task to summarize instructions on key issues, either in their own words or by repeating them. Graded in a manner that these defense-oriented scholars thought generous, the median score on this test was 5%; the mean was 9%. Thirty percent of jurors scored zero, and the highest score for any juror was 67%. In a real trial, with unlimited time for deliberation, jurors might give more attention to the instructions, and if they attended to them or argued about them, they might come to understand them better. Or they might not.

Page 734. After note 8, add:

8.1. In Barnes v. Gorman, 536 U.S. 181 (2002), the Court held that punitive damages are unavailable in claims under §202 of the Americans with Disabilities Act, 42 U.S.C. §12132 (2000), and §504 of the Rehabilitation Act, 29 U.S.C. §794(a) (2000). These laws prohibit discrimination on the basis of disability, and they borrow their remedies from the remedies available under an implied cause of action to enforce Title VI of the Civil Rights Act of 1964, 42 U.S.C. §2000d (2000). Title VI is a Spending Clause provision; it says that no program or activity that accepts federal financial assistance may discriminate on the basis of race. This is the key point; the case is about remedies for violating conditions attached to federal financial assistance. You can ignore or forget the details of the three statutory provisions.

The claim was against certain municipal officials in Kansas City in their official capacity. The Court held that conditional financial assistance is like a contract: programs that accept federal money agree to comply with various federal laws, and failure to comply is like a breach of contract. And punitive damages are historically unavailable for breach of contract.

The Court did not rely on *Newport*, probably because it viewed its Spending Clause theory as a bigger contribution to its growing federalism jurisprudence. Justice Scalia wrote the opinion in *Barnes*, and it goes far to vindicate one of his earlier opinions, concurring in the result and trying to narrow the majority's rationale. That issue is described in the supplement to page 1051. The Court was unanimous on the result in *Barnes*, but three Justices rejected the rationale and would have relied on *Newport*.

Page 736. After note 11, add:

12. A team at Cornell has studied punitive damages with the combined 1992, 1996, and 2001 data sets from the Justice Department studies cited in the main volume at 735. Theodore Eisenberg, Paula L. Hannaford-Agor, Michel Heise, Neil LaFountain, G. Thomas Munsterman, Brian Ostrom & Martin T. Wells, *Juries, Judges, and Punitive Damages: Empirical Analyses Using the Civil Justice Survey of State Courts 1992, 1996, and 2001 Data*, 3 J. of Empirical Legal Stud. 263 (2006). Out of 11,610 trials with a plaintiff win, they found 551 awards of punitive damages, or 4.75%. Plaintiffs win about half of all cases, so that's about 2.4% of cases tried. About 97% of cases settle, so about 7 of every 10,000 cases filed in large urban counties end in an award of punitive damages.

Of the punitives awarded, 24% of awards were under $10,000, and 60% were under $100,000; just under 11% were over $1 million. There was a strong correlation between the amount of compensatories and the amount of punitives, and strong similarities in the behavior of judges and juries. Judges and juries awarded punitives in similar percentages of cases, and their median awards were about the same. But the mean jury award was higher, reflecting the greater frequency of unusually large jury awards.

Page 736. After note 1, add:

1.1. The studies by Sunstein *et al.* found very high agreement on the moral culpability of defendant's conduct. Presented with a range of personal injury cases, and individually asked to rate the outrageousness of defendant's behavior on a scale from zero to six, the correlations among potential jurors exceeded .9, a result that is almost unheard of in social science research. Asked to rank ten cases in order of outrageousness, the correlation reached .99! (The theoretical limit, if every potential juror exactly agreed with every other, is 1.00.) These correlations persisted across variations in race and ethnicity, geography, income, and education. Correlations presumably would have been lower, perhaps much lower, if potential jurors had been asked to rate cases with different categories of misconduct -- say one personal injury case, one race discrimination case, one consumer fraud case, and one wrongful discharge case.

In the actual studies, agreement broke down at the stage of assigning a dollar value to punishment. Correlations among individual assessments dropped to .42, and the range was enormous. The researchers estimated that the 90th percentile verdict was 7.7 times larger than the median verdict in the same case, which in turn was 6.6 times larger than the 10th percentile verdict.

The researchers asked each potential juror to individually decide the case and set an amount of punitive damages. Then the potential jurors were assembled into mock juries and told to deliberate and reach a unanimous verdict if possible. Jury deliberations neither reduced variability nor produced results tending toward the middle of the individual awards. Deliberations produced far more variability, and generally higher verdicts, as compared to statistically combining the individual awards of the jurors participating in the deliberations. More than 27% of juries awarded as much or more than the highest individual award before deliberation; 83% awarded more than the median of the individual awards before deliberation.

These conclusions have been subject to especially telling criticisms on the ground that the case summaries provided little information from the defense. In a real jury deliberation, those jurors inclined to award smaller amounts would be armed with facts and arguments from defense counsel; in the simulations, such jurors had little or nothing to work with. It is a common result in social psychology experiments that discussion leads the group to more extreme conclusions, but this result is stronger, and far more likely to occur, when all the members of the group agree at the beginning or when only one-sided information is available.

Page 736. After note 2, add:

Engle was reversed on this and other grounds. The court of appeals said that punitives must be based on net worth, that judgments must be paid immediately, and that it is prejudicial to suggest to a jury that a judgment might be paid in installments. Liggett Group Inc. v. Engle, 853 So.2d 434 (Fla. Ct. App. 2003). On further appeal, the state supreme court relied on Florida precedent holding that punitive damages cannot exceed ability to pay, noted that the awards exceeded "the financial worth assigned to each company" by *plaintiffs'* expert, and concluded that this fact alone "clearly demonstrates that the award would result in an unlawful crippling of the defendant companies." Engle v. Liggett Group Inc., 945 So.2d 1246, 1265 n.8 (2006), *cert. filed*, 75 U.S.L.W. 3669 (May 21, 2007, No. 06-1545). Meanwhile, the Supreme Court has said that wealth can never be used to increase punitives above what would otherwise be constitutional limits. State Farm Mutual Automobile Insurance Co. v. Campbell, 538 U.S. 408 (2003), excerpted in the supplement to page 741.

Page 737. After note 3, add:

State Farm was belatedly reported at 65 P.3d 1134 (Utah 2001), and reversed on constitutional grounds, 538 U.S. 408 (2003). The constitutional opinion is excerpted in the supplement to page 741.

Page 738. After note 6, add:

6.1. For a collection of recent cases illustrating the variant rules on whether compensatories are prerequisite to punitives, see Cush-Crawford v. Adchem Corp., 271 F.3d 352 (2d Cir. 2001). *Cush-*

Crawford upheld $100,000 in punitives, with no compensatories, in a statutory sexual harassment case.

2. The Constitution

Page 739. After note 2, add:

2.1. The Ohio court ordered a similar division of punitive damages on its own authority. Dardinger v. Anthem Blue Cross & Blue Shield, 781 N.E.2d 121 (Ohio 2002). The case involved a $49-million punitive damages award against an insurer that refused to pay for treatment for a brain cancer patient, and stalled and misrepresented facts about its appeal procedures to both the patient's family and her medical providers. The court upheld the constitutionality of the $49 million, but found it excessive under state law and remitted it to $30 million. Then it said:

> At the punitive damages level, it is the societal element that is most important. The plaintiff remains a party, but the de facto party is our society, and the jury is determining whether and to what extent we as a society should punish the defendant.
>
> There is a philosophical void between the reasons we award punitive damages and how the damages are distributed. The community makes the statement, while the plaintiff reaps the monetary award.

Id. at 145. Noting that plaintiffs should have adequate incentive to litigate, it ordered that $10 million be paid to plaintiff, that attorneys fees be paid out of the remainder, based on the contingent fee contract and based on the full $30 million plus post-judgment interest, and that the remainder should be used to endow an Esther Dardinger Fund for cancer research at The Ohio State University.

Defendant paid the judgment and did not file a petition for certiorari. The case was decided after BMW v. Gore, discussed below, and while State Farm v. Campbell, also discussed below was pending in the Supreme Court.

2.2. Legislative and judicial experimentation with awarding a share of all punitives to the state are reviewed at length in Catherine M. Sharkey, *Punitive Damages as Societal Damages*, 113 Yale L.J. 347, 372-389, 414-440 (2003). The statutes vary considerably in their details. Some permit the state to intervene, and some do not; some give the money to the state treasury, some to special funds for various purposes. A sixth such statute has now been upheld.

Professor Sharkey views these statutes as a first step in the direction of her own ambitious proposal to reconceptualize punitive damages as compensatory damages for other persons injured by defendant's pattern of illegal conduct. She hopes to use punitive damage class actions to determine the amount of such "societal" compensation, which would be paid into a fund from which other victims could collect by filing an administrative claim. The practical and due process obstacles seem enormous, but she takes those obstacles seriously and sketches out possible procedures. Recent cases in the Supreme Court, excerpted and reprinted below, seem to go in the opposite direction.

Page 741. Replace note 6, *BMW v. Gore*, and Notes on the Constitutionality of Punitive Damages, with the following:

NOTES ON *BMW v. GORE* AND ITS AFTERMATH

1. In BMW, Inc. v. Gore, 517 U.S. 559 (1996), the Court finally invalidated a punitive damages award on the ground that it was excessive. A new BMW arrived in the United States with a damaged finish, perhaps because of acid rain somewhere in shipment from Germany. BMW repainted the car and sold it without disclosing the repair. Statutes in about half the states required disclosure of substantial pre-sale repairs; the most stringent of these statutes required disclosure of repairs costing more than 3% of the value of the car. BMW based its national policy on this 3% threshold: it would sell the car as used if pre-sale repairs exceeded 3% of the car's retail value, and it did not disclose smaller repairs.

Nine months after the purchase, the buyer took the car to a Mr. Slick at Slick Finish, to get a finish treatment that would create a "snazzier appearance." Mr. Slick detected that the car had been repainted. An Alabama jury found common law fraud in BMW's nondisclosure, awarded $4,000 in compensatory damages for the reduced value of the car, and awarded $4,000,000 in punitive damages. The punitives apparently represented $4,000 per car times approximately 1,000 cars nationwide that had been repainted and sold without disclosure. This was not a class action; the $4,000,000 went to the individual plaintiff.

Only 14 of the 1,000 sales had been in Alabama. BMW argued that plaintiff had not shown that the out-of-state sales were illegal in the states where they occurred, and therefore that punitive damages could not be based on these sales. The Alabama Supreme Court agreed and reduced the award to $2,000,000.

The Supreme Court of the United States agreed that Alabama could not award punitives for the purpose of changing BMW's policy in other states, and that any award "must be supported by the State's interest in protecting its own consumers and its own economy." 517 U.S. at 572. The Court said that evidence of similar out-of-state conduct remained "relevant to the determination of the degree of reprehensibility of the defendant's conduct," *id.* at 574 n.21, but that any award must be based "solely on conduct that occurred within Alabama." *Id.* at 573-574. It is not clear what juries will make of this distinction, but at least the out-of-state incidents could be used to show that the in-state incidents were authorized by a deliberate policy. The distinction also has at least one other clear consequence: the number of out-of-state incidents could not be used as a multiplier. *Id.* n.21.

The Court announced three "guideposts" for assessing the constitutionality of punitive damage awards: "the degree of reprehensibility of the defendant's conduct"; the ratio "between the punitive damages award and *the harm likely to result* from the defendant's conduct as well as the harm that actually has occurred;" and "the civil or criminal penalties that could be imposed for comparable misconduct." *Id.* at 575, 581, 583. The Court found a low degree of reprehensibility (no risk of physical injury, and nondisclosure rather than misrepresentation); a 500:1 ratio of punitives to compensatories and no risk of other harm that might have happened but did not; and a maximum fine of $2,000 for one violation of the Alabama Deceptive Trade Practices Act. It vacated the award as "grossly excessive." *Id.* at 585.

On remand, the Alabama court ordered a new trial unless plaintiff accepted a remittitur of all but $50,000 of the punitive damages awarded. BMW, Inc. v. Gore, 701 So.2d 507 (Ala. 1997). It selected $50,000 as in the range of other Alabama verdicts in cases of repaired cars being sold as new.

2. *BMW* was 5-4, replete with qualifying language and such soft formulations as ""[G]eneral concerns of reasonableness . . . properly enter into the constitutional calculus." It remained unclear what reasonableness as a constitutional standard would add to reasonableness as a common law standard. A constitutional standard makes possible federal review of state punitive damages judgments, but realistically, the Supreme Court can review only a handful of cases. Another difference is that *Haslip* has encouraged the state courts to create lists of factors to guide judicial review of punitive verdicts, such as the seven Alabama factors in *Haslip* itself. Those lists are typically different from the three constitutional factors listed in *BMW*. So now we get opinions marching through the state's seven (or however many) common law factors, and then starting over and marching through the three federal constitutional factors. It has been harder to say whether these dual reviews actually affect results.

3. Another difference between common law and constitutional review emerged in Cooper Industries, Inc. v. Leatherman Tool Group, Inc., 532 U.S. 424 (2001). On a common law argument that punitive damages are excessive, federal courts of appeals should review only the trial judge's ruling on the motion to set aside the verdict, and review that only for abuse of discretion. But on an argument that punitive damages are unconstitutionally excessive, federal courts of appeals are to review the jury verdict de novo. It would seem to follow that the district judge should also assess the verdict de novo on a constitutional challenge. So one clear effect of the constitutional standard is to empower judges as against jurors, and appellate judges as against trial judges, and to give defendants multiple chances for de novo review of the verdict. The opinion is not clear whether this de novo standard is a constitutional requirement, applicable in state court as well, or a federal procedural rule applicable only in federal court, but state courts are reading it as

applicable to constitutional challenges in state court. Some of the cases are collected in Mosing v. Domas, 830 So.2d 967, 973 (La. 2002); a more recent example is Engle v. Liggett Group, Inc., 945 So.2d 1246, 1263 (Fla. 2006), *cert. filed*, 75 U.S.L.W. 3669 (May 21, 2007, No. 06-1545).

4. Another emerging difference is that when a court holds an award of punitive damages unconstitutionally excessive, the right to jury trial is not implicated and no remittitur is required. That is, plaintiff is not entitled to a new trial if he rejects the lower amount offered by the court; the court can simply enter judgment on the lower amount. Courts have said that the constitutional maximum is not a fact to be found by a jury, and that any larger verdict on retrial would again have to be rejected. Some of the state and federal cases are collected in Simon v. San Paolo U.S. Holding Co., Inc., 113 P.3d 63, 81 (Cal. 2005). Compare the very different constitutional rule long applied to common law decisions that a verdict is excessive, described in the main volume at pages 189-190.

NOTES ON *STATE FARM v. CAMPBELL* AND ITS AFTERMATH

1. The Court tightened its review of punitive damages in State Farm Mutual Automobile Insurance Co. v. Campbell, 538 U.S. 408 (2003). Campbell tried to pass six vans on a two-lane highway, causing an accident that killed one driver and permanently disabled another. He had $50,000 in liability insurance with State Farm. State Farm inexplicably refused to settle for the policy limits, and in a suit by the other two drivers, a jury awarded $186,000 against Campbell. Having assured Campbell and his wife that they had nothing to worry about and did not need separate counsel, State Farm now told them to put their house up for sale to help pay the judgment, and it refused to post a supersedeas bond that would delay collection pending appeal. Campbell eventually settled with the other two drivers by assigning them 90% of his bad-faith-refusal-to-settle claim against State Farm. After an unsuccessful appeal in the negligence case, State Farm paid the entire $186,000 judgment.

At the trial of the bad-faith claim, the evidence showed that State Farm set corporate financial goals that required capping the amounts it would pay on claims, without regard to the number of claims or their merit. To meet these caps, State Farm often refused to pay claims by, or settle claims against, unsophisticated insureds who were thought unlikely to be able to complain effectively. Reviewing the jury verdict on post-trial motions, the trial judge found ample evidence that State Farm's "Performance, Planning and Review" policy (PP & R) "functioned, and continues to function, as an unlawful scheme . . . to deny benefits owed consumers by paying out less than fair value in order to meet preset, arbitrary payout targets designed to enhance corporate profits." In pursuit of this scheme, State Farm put false documents in claim files, removed documents that suggested liability, and destroyed claims-handling manuals that might reveal the scheme. Former State Farm employees testified to the scheme, and one former employee provided a copy of the 1979 PP & R manual, in which the scheme had originated.

A jury awarded the Campbells $2.6 million in compensatory damages (mostly for emotional distress during the year-and-a-half they were subject to the judgment they could not begin to pay), plus $145 million in punitives. The trial judge reduced these awards to $1 million in compensatories and $25 million in punitives.

The Utah Supreme Court affirmed the reduced compensatory award but reinstated the full $145 million in punitives. It reasoned that the scheme was highly reprehensible, that State Farm had massive wealth, and that State Farm's "clandestine" actions would be punished "at most in one out of every 50,000 cases." 65 P.3d at 1153. State Farm could have faced civil and criminal penalties of $10,000 for each act of fraud, suspension of its license to conduct business in Utah, disgorgement of profits, and imprisonment of officers or employees.

2. The Supreme Court of the United States held that Utah could punish State Farm's treatment of the Campbells, but not State Farm's nationwide PP & R scheme.

A State cannot punish a defendant for conduct that may have been lawful where it occurred. *BMW*. Nor, as a general rule, does a State have a legitimate concern in imposing punitive damages to punish a defendant for unlawful acts committed outside of the State's jurisdiction. Any proper adjudication of conduct that occurred outside Utah to other persons would require their inclusion, and, to those parties, the Utah courts, in the usual case, would need to apply the laws of their relevant jurisdiction.

. . . A jury must be instructed, furthermore, that it may not use evidence of out-of-state conduct to punish a defendant for action that was lawful in the jurisdiction where it occurred. *BMW*. . . .

For a more fundamental reason, however, the Utah courts erred in relying upon this and other evidence: The courts awarded punitive damages to punish and deter conduct that bore no relation to the Campbells' harm. A defendant's dissimilar acts, independent from the acts upon which liability was premised, may not serve as the basis for punitive damages. A defendant should be punished for the conduct that harmed the plaintiff, not for being an unsavory individual or business. Due process does not permit courts, in the calculation of punitive damages, to adjudicate the merits of other parties' hypothetical claims against a defendant under the guise of the reprehensibility analysis, but we have no doubt the Utah Supreme Court did that here.
. . .

The Campbells have identified scant evidence of repeated misconduct of the sort that injured them. Nor does our review of the Utah courts' decisions convince us that State Farm was only punished for its actions toward the Campbells. Although evidence of other acts need not be identical to have relevance in the calculation of punitive damages, the Utah court erred here because evidence pertaining to claims that had nothing to do with a third-party lawsuit was introduced at length. . . . The Campbells' attempt to justify the courts' reliance upon this unrelated testimony on the theory that each dollar of profit made by underpaying a third-party claimant is the same as a dollar made by underpaying a first-party one. . . . The reprehensibility guidepost does not permit courts to expand the scope of the case so that a defendant may be punished for any malfeasance, which in this case extended for a 20-year period. In this case, because the Campbells have shown no conduct by State Farm similar to that which harmed them, the conduct that harmed them is the only conduct relevant to the reprehensibility analysis.

538 U.S. at 421-424.

3. The Court also tightened its review of the ratio between punitives and compensatories.

We decline again to impose a bright-line ratio which a punitive damages award cannot exceed. Our jurisprudence and the principles it has now established demonstrate, however, that, in practice, few awards exceeding a single-digit ratio between punitive and compensatory damages, to a significant degree, will satisfy due process. In *Haslip,* in upholding a punitive damages award, we concluded that an award of more than four times the amount of compensatory damages might be close to the line of constitutional impropriety. We cited that 4-to-1 ratio again in *BMW.* The Court further referenced a long legislative history, dating back over 700 years and going forward to today, providing for sanctions of double, treble, or quadruple damages to deter and punish. While these ratios are not binding, they are instructive. They demonstrate what should be obvious: Single-digit multipliers are more likely to comport with due process, while still achieving the State's goals of deterrence and retribution, than awards with ratios in range of 500 to 1, or, in this case, of 145 to 1.

Nonetheless, because there are no rigid benchmarks that a punitive damages award may not surpass, ratios greater than those we have previously upheld may comport with due process where "a particularly egregious act has resulted in only a small amount of economic damages." *BMW,* 517 U.S. at 582; see also *id.* (positing that a higher ratio *might* be necessary where "the injury is hard to detect or the monetary value of noneconomic harm might have been difficult to determine"). The converse is also true, however. When compensatory damages are substantial, then a lesser ratio, perhaps only equal to compensatory damages, can reach the outermost limit of the due process guarantee. The precise award in any case, of course, must be based upon the facts and circumstances of the defendant's conduct and the harm to the plaintiff.

Id. at 425.

4. The Court rejected the relevance of other factors the Utah court had relied on.

Here the argument that State Farm will be punished in only the rare case, coupled with reference to its assets (which, of course, are what other insured parties in Utah and other States must rely upon for payment of claims) had little to do with the actual harm sustained by the Campbells. The wealth of a defendant cannot justify an otherwise unconstitutional punitive damages award.

Id. at 427.

5. The award was also out of proportion to legislatively imposed penalties.

The most relevant civil sanction under Utah state law for the wrong done to the Campbells appears to be a $10,000 fine for an act of fraud, an amount dwarfed by the $145 million punitive damages award. The Supreme Court of Utah speculated about the loss of State Farm's business license, the disgorgement of profits, and possible imprisonment, but here again its references were to the broad fraudulent scheme drawn from evidence of out-of-state and dissimilar conduct. This analysis was insufficient to justify the award.

Id. at 428.

6. Justices Scalia and Thomas dissented on the ground that the Due Process Clause imposes no substantive limits on punitive damage awards. Justice Ginsburg agreed that limits on punitive damages should be left to state courts and legislatures. But her dissent also reviewed the evidence in much more detail than the

Court had done, and convincingly argued that the treatment of the Campbells was typical of State Farm's PP & R policy, and that much of State Farm's conduct, both inside and outside of Utah, was quite similar to what State Farm did to the Campbells.

7. On remand, the Utah court awarded $9 million in punitive damages. State Farm Mutual Automobile Insurance Co. v. Campbell, 98 P.3d 409 (Utah 2004). It viewed the case as deserving the highest ratio the U.S. Supreme Court had approved. It chose nine times compensatories, because nine is the highest single-digit number.

7. A wrongful death and permanent disability suffered by the other two drivers were worth only $185,859 to a Utah jury; the Campbells' emotional distress was worth $2.6 million, and $1 million after the trial court's remittitur. Is this disparity just the hazard of different juries hearing different cases? The difference between how juries assess damages against individual defendants and how they assess damages against corporate defendants? Or does it support the Supreme Court's suggestion that much of the compensatory award was really punitive?

8. *BMW* and *State Farm* both relied on the same three guideposts, and both invalidated enormous verdicts (especially when the *BMW* verdict is considered in light of the underlying wrong). One might say there was little new in *State Farm*. But the tone of the opinion was very different. The review of the facts was more intrusive; the suggested ratios came closer to bright-line rules; there was a new suggestion of a one-to-one ratio when compensatories are large. *State Farm* put the *BMW* guideposts on steroids. The majority increased from five to six (Chief Justice Rehnquist had been a persistent dissenter), and there was neither conciliatory language nor separate concurrences to suggest any difficulty in holding that majority together.

9. Many courts responded to *State Farm* by reducing punitive awards to single-digit ratios to compensatories. A preference for round numbers have led some to say that ten is not significantly different from nine (or 9.999). Others have noted that what the Court actually said is that "few" awards -- not none -- would be upheld if the ratio exceeded single digits "to a significant degree," and that

higher ratios might be justified where "a particularly egregious act has resulted in only a small amount of economic damages."

10. Judge Posner found such a case in Mathias v. Accor Economy Lodging, Inc., 347 F.3d 672 (7th Cir. 2003). Defendant operated a Motel 6 in downtown Chicago, charging more than $100 per night. The hotel was infested with bedbugs, but management refused to treat more aggressively, continued renting rooms, and misrepresented conditions. Plaintiffs were hotel guests bitten by bedbugs. "Although bedbug bites are not as serious as the bites of some other insects, they are painful and unsightly." *Id.* at 675. The jury awarded $5,000 in compensatories and $186,000 in punitives; the hotel had 191 rooms. The court upheld the award. "The defendant's behavior was outrageous but the compensable harm done was slight and at the same time difficult to quantify because a large element of it was emotional." *Id.* at 677. The small amount of damages justified a larger multiplier, in part so there would be a prospect of a sufficient judgment to attract counsel on a contingent fee basis. For commentary on *Mathias*, see Colleen P. Murphy, *The "Bedbug" Case and State Farm v. Campbell*, 9 Roger Williams U.L. Rev. 579 (2004).

Many were bitten but few had sued -- perhaps no one else. Increasing punishment in response to low odds that the punishment will be inflicted is such a cherished law-and-economics idea that Posner relied on it without noting any question about it. But didn't *State Farm* reject that idea?

11. Another such case is Kemp v. American Telephone & Telegraph Co., 393 F.3d 1354 (11th Cir. 2004). Plaintiff's grandson ran up $115 in charges at a 900 number, playing a game called "Let's Make a Deal," at $3.88 a minute. Players who spent long enough on the call had one chance in 2700 of winning a $2000 prize, so the game violated Georgia's gambling laws. The $3.88 a minute went to the gaming company, but AT&T billed it as a long-distance charge, and the deceptive billing was essential to the gaming business. The jury found fraud and awarded $1 million in punitives.

Treating five indicia of reprehensibility mentioned in *State Farm* as a five-factors test, the court of appeals found three of them present: AT&T's conduct was deceitful, it was repeated, and it targeted the financially vulnerable. The court appeared to treat the other two factors -- physical harm and reckless indifference to health or safety -- as not relevant to the case rather than as not satisfied. Concluding that the conduct was reprehensible, that nine times $115 would be trivial to AT&T, and that wealth remains relevant to application of the three *State Farm* guideposts, the court allowed $250,000 of the punitives to stand.

12. "The wealth of a defendant cannot justify an otherwise unconstitutional punitive damages award." Does that mean wealth is wholly irrelevant to the constitutional analysis? Does it mean evidence of wealth is no longer admissible? Certainly the Court never says that explicitly. And *Kemp* is not the only case to say that defendant's wealth still has some role to play in influencing the analysis of the three guideposts. Perhaps wealth becomes relevant after the court decides that this is one of the cases with substantial reprehensibility and small compensatory damages.

Might it still be unconstitutional to award more than defendants' wealth, or too large a percentage of defendants' wealth? See Engle v. Liggett Group Inc., 945 So.2d 1246, 1265 n.8 (Fla. 2006), *cert. filed*, 75 U.S.L.W. 3669 (May 21, 2007, No. 06-1545) (further described in main volume and supplement at pages 731 and 736), rejecting punitives in excess of net worth on state law grounds. Can it be that wealth is relevant to limit punitives but not to increase them?

Judge Posner thought wealth was relevant only because it empowered a tenacious and even frivolous defense, thus increasing the difficulty of finding a lawyer. He also offered the unsolicited advice, "the parties having made nothing of the point," that net worth "is an accounting artifact" and "not the correct measure of a corporation's resources." A firm financed with debt may have the same size and resources as a firm financed with equity, but their net worth will be very different. *Mathias*, 347 F.3d at 677-678.

13. The Third Circuit held that an award of attorneys' fees can be the denominator in calculating the ratio of punitive damages to compensatory awards. Willow Inn, Inc. v. Public Service Mutual Insurance Co., 399 F.3d 224 (3d Cir. 2005). Despite long and unjustified delays, the insured ultimately recovered for tornado damage to its building before filing a lawsuit. It then sued for bad faith failure to settle, recovering $2,000 in compensatory damages for a single unpaid claim, $135,000 in attorneys' fees (apparently

incurred in the bad faith suit, not in the prelitigation pursuit of the insurance claim), and $150,000 in punitive damages. The court held the punitives not excessive when compared to the fees, relying in part on a Pennsylvania decision holding that fee awards under the state's insurance bad faith statute were a form of compensatory damages for this purpose.

14. The Connecticut court has upheld an arbitration award of no compensatories and $5-million punitives. MedValUSA Health Programs, Inc. v. Memberworks, Inc., 872 A.2d 423 (Conn. 2005). The court said the arbitrator's award, even when judicially enforced, is not state action and not subject to the Due Process Clause. The arbitrator's explanation for the infinite ratio of punitives to compensatories was that plaintiff proved numerous unfair and deceptive practices but failed to prove damages with reasonable certainty.

15. The teeth of the *State Farm* opinion was in its holding that nearly all of State Farm's other misconduct was irrelevant. This implied a very tight definition of what misconduct is sufficiently analogous to count. It seemed to require proof of specific Utah examples, rejecting the inference that a policy promulgated and implemented nationally must have been applied in Utah as well. The Court seemed concerned about multiple liability if the same pattern of misconduct is used to prove reprehensibility in multiple cases. But it will be very much harder to prove reprehensibility without showing a pattern that suggests a policy coming down from the top. The Court returned to the problem of related wrongdoing in the next case.

PHILIP MORRIS CO. v. WILLIAMS
127 S.Ct. 1057 (2007)

Justice BREYER delivered the opinion of the Court.

[Plaintiff's decedent died of lung cancer after smoking Marlboros for 40 years. The theory of the case was fraud -- that Philip Morris knew for the entire 40 years that there was at least a substantial risk that smoking caused cancer, and knew for most of that time that smoking in fact caused cancer, but that it falsely and systematically sought to reassure the public and minimize the risk so that people would keep smoking. When his family tried to persuade him to quit smoking, Williams had repeated the industry's assurances that smoking was safe. The jury awarded $21,000 in "economic" damages -- Williams died soon after his diagnosis, so his medical expenses were modest, and if he was retired, there may have been no lost income -- $800,000 in "noneconomic" damages, and $79.5 million in punitives. The "noneconomic" damages were reduced to $500,000 in compliance with a statutory cap.

Plaintiff's attorney emphasized all the other Oregon smokers who had been deceived by the same ads. He told the jury to "think about how many other Jesse Williams in the last 40 years in the State of Oregon there have been. . . . In Oregon, how many people do we see outside, driving home . . . smoking cigarettes? . . . [C]igarettes . . . are going to kill ten [of every hundred]. [And] the market share of Marlboros [*i.e.,* Philip Morris] is one-third [*i.e.,* one of every three killed]." [Quotations selected and edited by Justice Breyer].

The Oregon court upheld the punitives after a close textual analysis of *State Farm*. It concluded that defendant's conduct was extremely reprehensible, intentionally inflicting substantial risk of serious illness or death on thousands of Oregonians. It read *State Farm* as forbidding punishment for out-of-state conduct or for conduct dissimilar to the illegal conduct directed at plaintiff, but as permitting punishment for conduct directed to others that was both in-state and similar. It said that the point of considering statutory civil and criminal penalties for the same conduct is not to find a dollar-for-dollar equivalence, but to see how seriously the legislature has treated this misconduct within the range of penalties provided by legislators. It concluded that what Philip Morris had done was manslaughter, a felony that the legislature treated very seriously. On the other hand, it acknowledged that the punitives far exceeded a single-digit ratio to compensatories, either before or after the reduction to the statutory cap. But it said that the single-digit ratio is not a rigid rule; single-digit ratios can be exceeded when the conduct is unusually reprehensible, and this was such a case.]

II

This Court has long made clear that "[p]unitive damages may properly be imposed to further a State's legitimate interests in punishing unlawful conduct and deterring its repetition." *BMW*, 517 U.S. at 568. See also Gertz v. Robert Welch, Inc., 418 U.S. 323 (1974); City of Newport v. Fact Concerts, Inc., 453 U.S. 247 (1981); Pacific Mutual Life Ins. Co. v. Haslip, 499 U.S. 1 (1991). At the same time, we have emphasized the need to avoid an arbitrary determination of an award's amount. Unless a State insists upon proper standards that will cabin the jury's discretionary authority, its punitive damages system may deprive a defendant of "fair notice . . . of the severity of the penalty that a State may impose," *BMW*, 517 U.S. at 574; it may threaten "arbitrary punishments," *i.e.,* punishments that reflect not an "application of law" but "a decisionmaker's caprice," *State Farm*, 538 U.S. at 416; and, where the amounts are sufficiently large, it may impose one State's (or one jury's) "policy choice," say as to the conditions under which (or even whether) certain products can be sold, upon "neighboring States" with different public policies, *BMW*, 517 U.S. at 571-572.

For these and similar reasons, this Court has found that the Constitution imposes certain limits, in respect both to procedures for awarding punitive damages and to amounts forbidden as "grossly excessive." See *Honda Motor*, 512 U.S. at 432 (1994) (requiring judicial review of the size of punitive awards); *Cooper Industries*, (review must be *de novo*); *BMW* (excessiveness decision depends upon the reprehensibility of the defendant's conduct, whether the award bears a reasonable relationship to the actual and potential harm caused by the defendant to the plaintiff, and the difference between the award and sanctions "authorized or imposed in comparable cases"); *State Farm* (excessiveness more likely where ratio exceeds single digits). Because we shall not decide whether the award here at issue is "grossly excessive," we need now only consider the Constitution's procedural limitations.

III

In our view, the Constitution's Due Process Clause forbids a State to use a punitive damages award to punish a defendant for injury that it inflicts upon nonparties or those whom they directly represent, *i.e.,* injury that it inflicts upon those who are, essentially, strangers to the litigation. For one thing, the Due Process Clause prohibits a State from punishing an individual without first providing that individual with "an opportunity to present every available defense." Lindsey v. Normet, 405 U.S. 56, 66 (1972). Yet a defendant threatened with punishment for injuring a nonparty victim has no opportunity to defend against the charge, by showing, for example in a case such as this, that the other victim was not entitled to damages because he or she knew that smoking was dangerous or did not rely upon the defendant's statements to the contrary.

For another, to permit punishment for injuring a nonparty victim would add a near standardless dimension to the punitive damages equation. How many such victims are there? How seriously were they injured? Under what circumstances did injury occur? The trial will not likely answer such questions as to nonparty victims. The jury will be left to speculate. And the fundamental due process concerns to which our punitive damages cases refer -- risks of arbitrariness, uncertainty and lack of notice -- will be magnified. *State Farm*; *BMW*.

Finally, we can find no authority supporting the use of punitive damages awards for the purpose of punishing a defendant for harming others. We have said that it may be appropriate to consider the reasonableness of a punitive damages award in light of the *potential* harm the defendant's conduct could have caused. But we have made clear that the potential harm at issue was harm potentially caused *the plaintiff*. . . .

Respondent argues that she is free to show harm to other victims because it is relevant to a different part of the punitive damages constitutional equation, namely, reprehensibility. That is to say, harm to others shows more reprehensible conduct. Philip Morris, in turn, does not deny that a plaintiff may show harm to others in order to demonstrate reprehensibility. Nor do we.

Evidence of actual harm to nonparties can help to show that the conduct that harmed the plaintiff also posed a substantial risk of harm to the general public, and so was particularly reprehensible -- although counsel may argue in a particular case that conduct resulting in no harm to others nonetheless posed a grave risk to the public, or the converse. Yet for the reasons given above, a jury may not go further than this and use a punitive damages verdict to punish a defendant directly on account of harms it is alleged to have visited on nonparties.

Given the risks of unfairness that we have mentioned, it is constitutionally important for a court to provide assurance that the jury will ask the right question, not the wrong one. And given the risks of arbitrariness, the concern for adequate notice, and the risk that punitive damages awards can, in practice, impose one State's (or one jury's) policies (*e.g.,* banning cigarettes) upon other States -- all of which accompany awards that, today, may be many times the size of such awards in the 18th and 19th centuries -- it is particularly important that States avoid procedure that unnecessarily deprives juries of proper legal guidance. We therefore conclude that the Due Process Clause requires States to provide assurance that juries are not asking the wrong question, *i.e.,* seeking, not simply to determine reprehensibility, but also to punish for harm caused strangers.

IV

Respondent suggests as well that the Oregon Supreme Court, in essence, agreed with us, that it did not authorize punitive damages awards based upon punishment for harm caused to nonparties. We concede that one might read some portions of the Oregon Supreme Court's opinion as focusing only upon reprehensibility. See, *e.g.,* 127 P.3d at 1175 ("[T]he jury could consider whether Williams and his misfortune were merely exemplars of the harm that Philip Morris was prepared to inflict on the smoking public at large"). But the Oregon court's opinion elsewhere makes clear that that court held more than these few phrases might suggest.

The instruction that Philip Morris said the trial court should have given distinguishes between using harm to others as part of the "reasonable relationship" equation (which it would allow) and using it directly as a basis for punishment. The instruction asked the trial court to tell the jury that "you *may* consider the extent of harm suffered by others *in determining what [the] reasonable relationship is*" between Philip Morris' punishable misconduct and harm caused to Jesse Williams, *"[but] you are not to punish the defendant for the impact of its alleged misconduct on other persons, who may bring lawsuits of their own* in which other juries can resolve their claims" (emphasis added). And as the Oregon Supreme Court explicitly recognized, Philip Morris argued that the Constitution "prohibits the state, acting through a civil jury, from using punitive damages to punish a defendant for harm to nonparties."

The court rejected that claim. In doing so, it pointed out (1) that this Court in *State Farm* had held only that a jury could not base its award upon "dissimilar" acts of a defendant. It added (2) that "[i]f a jury cannot punish for the conduct, then it is difficult to see why it may consider it at all." And it stated (3) that "[i]t is unclear to us how a jury could 'consider' harm to others, yet withhold that consideration from the punishment calculus."

The Oregon court's first statement is correct. We did not previously hold explicitly that a jury may not punish for the harm caused others. But we do so hold now. We do not agree with the Oregon court's second statement. We have explained why we believe the Due Process Clause prohibits a State's inflicting punishment for harm caused strangers to the litigation. At the same time we recognize that conduct that risks harm to many is likely more reprehensible than conduct that risks harm to only a few. And a jury consequently may take this fact into account in determining reprehensibility. Cf., e.g., Witte v. United States, 515 U.S. 389, 400 (1995) (recidivism statutes taking into account a criminal defendant's other misconduct do not impose an "'additional penalty for the earlier crimes,' but instead . . . 'a stiffened penalty for the latest crime, which is considered to be an aggravated offense because a repetitive one'" (quoting Gryger v. Burke, 334 U.S. 728, 732 (1948).

The Oregon court's third statement raises a practical problem. How can we know whether a jury, in taking account of harm

119

caused others under the rubric of reprehensibility, also seeks to *punish* the defendant for having caused injury to others? Our answer is that state courts cannot authorize procedures that create an unreasonable and unnecessary risk of any such confusion occurring. In particular, we believe that where the risk of that misunderstanding is a significant one -- because, for instance, of the sort of evidence that was introduced at trial or the kinds of argument the plaintiff made to the jury -- a court, upon request, must protect against that risk. Although the States have some flexibility to determine what *kind* of procedures they will implement, federal constitutional law obligates them to provide *some* form of protection in appropriate cases.

V

As the preceding discussion makes clear, we believe that the Oregon Supreme Court applied the wrong constitutional standard when considering Philip Morris' appeal. We remand this case so that the Oregon Supreme Court can apply the standard we have set forth. Because the application of this standard may lead to the need for a new trial, or a change in the level of the punitive damages award, we shall not consider whether the award is constitutionally "grossly excessive." We vacate the Oregon Supreme Court's judgment and remand the case for further proceedings not inconsistent with this opinion. . . .

Justice STEVENS, dissenting.

The Due Process Clause of the Fourteenth Amendment imposes both substantive and procedural constraints on the power of the States to impose punitive damages on tortfeasors. See *State Farm*; *Cooper Industries*; *BMW*; *Honda Motor*; *TXO*. I remain firmly convinced that the cases announcing those constraints were correctly decided. In my view the Oregon Supreme Court faithfully applied the reasoning in those opinions to the egregious facts disclosed by this record. I agree with Justice Ginsburg's explanation of why no procedural error even arguably justifying reversal occurred at the trial in this case.

Of greater importance to me, however, is the Court's imposition of a novel limit on the State's power to impose punishment in civil litigation. Unlike the Court, I see no reason why an interest in punishing a wrongdoer "for harming persons who are not before the court" should not be taken into consideration when assessing the appropriate sanction for reprehensible conduct.

Whereas compensatory damages are measured by the harm the defendant has caused the plaintiff, punitive damages are a sanction for the public harm the defendant's conduct has caused or threatened. There is little difference between the justification for a criminal sanction, such as a fine or a term of imprisonment, and an award of punitive damages. See *Cooper Industries*. In our early history either type of sanction might have been imposed in litigation prosecuted by a private citizen. And while in neither context would the sanction typically include a pecuniary award measured by the harm that the conduct had caused to any third parties, in both contexts the harm to third parties would surely be a relevant factor to consider in evaluating the reprehensibility of the defendant's wrongdoing. We have never held otherwise.

In the case before us, evidence attesting to the possible harm the defendant's extensive deceitful conduct caused other Oregonians was properly presented to the jury. No evidence was offered to establish an appropriate measure of damages to compensate such third parties for their injuries, and no one argued that the punitive damages award would serve any such purpose. To award compensatory damages to remedy such third-party harm might well constitute a taking of property from the defendant without due process. But a punitive damages award, instead of serving a compensatory purpose, serves the entirely different purposes of retribution and deterrence that underlie every criminal sanction. *State Farm*. This justification for punitive damages has even greater salience when, as in this case, see Ore. Rev. Stat. §31.735(1) (2003), the award is payable in whole or in part to the State rather than to the private litigant.[1]

---

[1] The Court's holding in *Browning-Ferris Industries* distinguished, for the purposes of appellate review under the Excessive Fines Clause of the Eighth Amendment, between criminal sanctions and civil fines awarded entirely to the plaintiff. The fact that part of the award in this case is payable to the State lends further support to my conclusion that it should be treated as the functional

While apparently recognizing the novelty of its holding, the majority relies on a distinction between taking third-party harm into account in order to assess the reprehensibility of the defendant's conduct -- which is permitted -- from doing so in order to punish the defendant "directly" -- which is forbidden. This nuance eludes me. When a jury increases a punitive damages award because injuries to third parties enhanced the reprehensibility of the defendant's conduct, the jury is by definition punishing the defendant -- directly -- for third-party harm.[1] A murderer who kills his victim by throwing a bomb that injures dozens of bystanders should be punished more severely than one who harms no one other than his intended victim. Similarly, there is no reason why the measure of the appropriate punishment for engaging in a campaign of deceit in distributing a poisonous and addictive substance to thousands of cigarette smokers statewide should not include consideration of the harm to those "bystanders" as well as the harm to the individual plaintiff. The Court endorses a contrary conclusion without providing us with any reasoned justification.

It is far too late in the day to argue that the Due Process Clause merely guarantees fair procedure and imposes no substantive limits on a State's lawmaking power. It remains true, however, that the Court should be "reluctant to expand the concept of substantive due process because guideposts for responsible decisionmaking in this unchartered [sic] area are scarce and open-ended." Collins v. City of Harker Heights, 503 U.S. 115, 125 (1992). Judicial restraint counsels us to "exercise the utmost care whenever we are asked to break new ground in this field." Id. Today the majority ignores that sound advice when it announces its new rule of

---

equivalent of a criminal sanction. I continue to agree with Justice O'Connor and those scholars who have concluded that the Excessive Fines Clause is applicable to punitive damages awards regardless of who receives the ultimate payout.

[1] It is no answer to refer, as the majority does, to recidivism statutes. In that context, we have distinguished between taking prior crimes into account as an aggravating factor in penalizing the conduct before the court versus doing so to punish for the earlier crimes. But if enhancing a penalty for a present crime because of prior conduct that has already been punished is permissible, it is certainly proper to enhance a penalty because the conduct before the court, which has never been punished, injured multiple victims.

substantive law.

Essentially for the reasons stated in the opinion of the Supreme Court of Oregon, I would affirm its judgment.

Justice THOMAS, dissenting.

I join Justice Ginsburg's dissent in full. I write separately to reiterate my view that "'the Constitution does not constrain the size of punitive damages awards.'" *State Farm*, 538 U.S. at 429-30 (Thomas, J., dissenting) (quoting *Cooper Industries*, 532 U.S. at 443 (Thomas, J., concurring). It matters not that the Court styles today's holding as "procedural" because the "procedural" rule is simply a confusing implementation of the substantive due process regime this Court has created for punitive damages. See *Haslip*, 499 U.S. at 26-27 (Scalia, J., concurring in judgment) ("In 1868 . . . punitive damages were undoubtedly an established part of the American common law of torts. It is . . . clear that no particular procedures were deemed necessary to circumscribe a jury's discretion regarding the award of such damages, or their amount"). Today's opinion proves once again that this Court's punitive damages jurisprudence is "insusceptible of principled application." *BMW*, 517 U.S. at 599 (Scalia J., joined by Thomas J., dissenting).

Justice GINSBURG, with whom Justices SCALIA and THOMAS join, dissenting.

The purpose of punitive damages, it can hardly be denied, is not to compensate, but to punish. Punish for what? Not for harm actually caused "strangers to the litigation," the Court states, but for the *reprehensibility* of defendant's conduct. "[C]onduct that risks harm to many," the Court observes, "is likely more reprehensible than conduct that risks harm to only a few." The Court thus conveys that, when punitive damages are at issue, a jury is properly instructed to consider the extent of harm suffered by others as a measure of reprehensibility, but not to mete out punishment for injuries in fact sustained by nonparties. The Oregon courts did not rule otherwise. They have endeavored to follow our decisions, most recently in *BMW* and *State Farm*, and have "deprive[d] [no jury] of proper legal guidance." Vacation of the Oregon Supreme Court's judgment, I am convinced, is unwarranted.

The right question regarding reprehensibility, the Court acknowledges, would train on "the harm that Philip Morris was prepared to inflict on the smoking public at large." See also 127 P.3d at 1177 ("[T]he jury, *in assessing the reprehensibility of Philip Morris's actions,* could consider evidence of similar harm to other Oregonians caused (or threatened) by the same conduct" (emphasis added)). The Court identifies no evidence introduced and no charge delivered inconsistent with that inquiry.

The Court's order vacating the Oregon Supreme Court's judgment is all the more inexplicable considering that Philip Morris did not preserve any objection to the charges in fact delivered to the jury, to the evidence introduced at trial, or to opposing counsel's argument. The sole objection Philip Morris preserved was to the trial court's refusal to give defendant's requested charge number 34. The proposed instruction read in pertinent part:

> If you determine that some amount of punitive damages should be imposed on the defendant, it will then be your task to set an amount that is appropriate. This should be such amount as you believe is necessary to achieve the objectives of deterrence and punishment. While there is no set formula to be applied in reaching an appropriate amount, I will now advise you of some of the factors that you may wish to consider in this connection.

> (1) The size of any punishment should bear a reasonable relationship to the harm caused to Jesse Williams by the defendant's punishable misconduct. Although you may consider the extent of harm suffered by others in determining what that reasonable relationship is, you are not to punish the defendant for the impact of its alleged misconduct on other persons, who may bring lawsuits of their own in which other juries can resolve their claims and award punitive damages for those harms, as such other juries see fit. . . .

> (2) The size of the punishment may appropriately reflect the degree of reprehensibility of the defendant's conduct --

that is, how far the defendant has departed from accepted societal norms of conduct.

Under that charge, just what use could the jury properly make of "the extent of harm suffered by others"? The answer slips from my grasp. A judge seeking to enlighten rather than confuse surely would resist delivering the requested charge.

The Court ventures no opinion on the propriety of the charge proposed by Philip Morris, though Philip Morris preserved no other objection to the trial proceedings. Rather than addressing the one objection Philip Morris properly preserved, the Court reaches outside the bounds of the case as postured when the trial court entered its judgment. I would accord more respectful treatment to the proceedings and dispositions of state courts that sought diligently to adhere to our changing, less than crystalline precedent. . . .

NOTES ON CONSTITUTIONAL LIMITS ON PUNITIVE DAMAGES

1. In *Philip Morris*, the other wrongdoing was not just in-state and similar; it was the very same conduct. The very same ad campaign that deceived Jesse Williams -- to some extent, the very same ads -- deceived other Oregon smokers. Unlike *State Farm*, *Philip Morris* is not about the degree of similarity of the other wrongdoing. It relies on a different distinction -- between punishing the other wrongdoing and using that other wrongdoing to assess the reprehensibility of defendant's treatment of the plaintiff. This distinction was prefigured in the Court's treatment of out-of-state wrongdoing in BMW v. Gore.

2. Will this make a difference in results? Or will it merely require a new jury instruction? The dissenters claimed not to understand the distinction; how will juries understand it? And how will courts review how the jury implemented the distinction?

3. Perhaps one operational consequence could be this: Other similar wrongdoing can help justify an award of nine times plaintiff's compensatories, instead of some smaller multiplier, but rarely anything more. If other wrongdoing can help justify a hundred times

plaintiff's compensatories, it is hard to see what the Court has accomplished. Some lawyers familiar with the case predict that the Oregon courts will reaffirm the original award on remand. But unless that holding is based on procedural default, wouldn't it require a new trial and a comparably large award of punitives by a properly instructed second jury?

4. Does *Philip Morris*'s limit on what juries can do with evidence of other wrongdoing replace or supplement *State Farm*'s stringent requirement of similarity between the wrongdoing aimed at plaintiff and any other wrongdoing considered? That is, if the jury is properly instructed not to punish other wrongdoing but simply to consider it as evidence of reprehensibility, does the other wrongdoing have to be so nearly identical?

5. Justices O'Connor and Stevens have long been essential votes in the Court's campaign to limit punitive damages; Chief Justice Rehnquist provided a new sixth vote in State Farm v. Campbell. But O'Connor and Rehnquist are now gone, and Stevens voted with the dissenters in *Philip Morris*. The majority was sustained by the two new justices, Roberts and Alito, who joined in extending the Court's precedents and showed no interest in the Scalia-Thomas view that these cases are substantive due process with no basis in the Constitution.

6. Asbestos manufacturers have long argued without success that multiple punitive damage awards take their property without due process. Most courts agreed in principle that there must be some aggregate constitutional limit on punitive damages for a series of related wrongful acts, but no court ever thought it had either a workable solution or a sufficient record to decide that that limit had been reached. Some of the cases are collected in Owens-Corning Fiberglas Corp. v. Malone, 972 S.W.2d 35 (Tex. 1998). At the time of trial, $52 million in punitive damages had been awarded against Owens-Corning, and Owens-Corning claimed that $14 million more had been awarded pending appeal. But only $3 million had been paid, and because most large punitive awards are reversed or reduced, the majority refused to count anything that had not yet been paid. Owens-Corning, which was telling courts that it faced confiscatory punitive damages, had told its stockholders that its future asbestos liability should have no material adverse effect on

the company. That was wrong; on October 5, 2000, Owens-Corning filed for bankruptcy.

7. The asbestos cases tried to let each victim prove the whole pattern of misconduct, and then somehow cap the total of all punitive awards based on that pattern. *State Farm* took a very different approach; it defined the relevant pattern so narrowly that the same pattern will not be proved in nearly as many cases. Assuming *State Farm* still matters after *Philip Morris*, are all sales of asbestos one pattern, or is asbestos insulation different from asbestos fireproofing? Is insulation around pipes different from insulation in walls? Is wall insulation different from ceiling insulation? Is insulating 8-inch pipes different from insulating 4-inch pipes? Or is there something special about the difference between first-party and third-party insurance, so that other products will be harder to subdivide?

3. Punitive Damages in Contract

Page 768. After note 10, add:

11. The Supreme Court of Virginia has denied punitive damages for legal malpractice. O'Connell v. Bean, 556 S.E.2d 741 (Va. 2002). Constructive fraud and breach of fiduciary duty were not independent torts; they were merely specifications of the duties created by the attorney-client contract. The court left open the possibility that an attorney might commit a tort that went beyond breaching her contractual duties.

In a distinct holding, the Supreme Court of California denied compensatory damages in the amount of the punitives that allegedly would have been collected but for defendant's legal malpractice. Ferguson v. Lieff, Cabraser, Heimann & Bernstein, LLP, 69 P.3d 965 (Cal. 2003). The court reasoned that plaintiffs had no entitlement to punitives, that the burdens of proof would be confusing to juries (did plaintiff prove by a preponderance of the evidence that a jury in the first case would have found by clear and convincing evidence . . .), and that the amounts would be wholly speculative. The opinion collects decisions going the other way with little consideration of whether to depart from the usual measure of damages.

B. OTHER PUNITIVE REMEDIES

1. Statutory Recoveries by Private Litigants

Page 768. After note 2, add:

The summary of the Truth in Lending Act contains an editorial blunder; the exceptional $200 and $2,000 minimum and maximum applies to closed-end loans secured by real property or a dwelling. The section has been repeatedly amended over the years, and it no longer says what Congress meant (although these drafting problems were not the source of my misreading in the main volume). When §1640(a) had two clauses ((i) and (ii)), the $100 and $1,000 minimum and maximum appeared at the end of the subparagraph and applied to both clauses. Then Congress added the exceptional $200 and $2,000 minimum and maximum in clause (iii), leaving the $100 and $1,000 maximum and minimum in clause (ii), where grammatically, it applied only to clause (ii). Clause (i), which covers most consumer loans, appeared to no longer have a minimum or a maximum. You can take my word for it, or you can look up the statute to see what happened, but the amended statute unambiguously said something quite different from what Congress had intended. The Supreme Court relied on the drafting history over the years to determine what Congress meant, and enforced what Congress meant instead of what it said. Koons Buick Pontiac GMC, Inc. v. Nigh, 543 U.S. 50 (2004). Justice Scalia dissented, insisting that the Court cannot fix Congress's drafting errors.

2.1. The Privacy Act provides that for certain intentional or willful violations, the United States shall be liable for "actual damages sustained by the individual as a result of the refusal or failure, but in no case shall *a person entitled to recovery* receive less than the sum of $1,000." 5 U.S.C. §552(g)(4)(A) (2000). The Court held that a plaintiff must prove some actual damages to collect the statutory minimum recovery. Doe v. Chao, 540 U.S. 614 (2004). There were three dissents, and much debate, but the heart of the majority opinion was that the words I have italicized require plaintiff to prove he is entitled to recovery before he can claim the $1,000. That is a plausible interpretation, but a very odd result (or perhaps a very odd statute). As the dissenting judge below pointed out, "minimum statutory damages" are "a fairly common feature of federal legislation." But he knew of no statute where Congress had provided for "a statutory minimum to actual damages." Doe v. Chao, 306 F.3d 170, 195 (4th Cir. 2002) (Michael, J., dissenting in part). Now there is one.

2. Civil Penalties Payable to the Government

Page 774. At the end of the first paragraph of note 7, add:

The Court rejected an Ex Post Facto Clause attack on an Alaska statute that required sex offenders, after their release from prison, to register with the state and have their photograph, address, license plate number, and other identifying information posted on the Internet. Smith v. Doe, 538 U.S. 84 (2003). The Court said this was remedial not punitive, intended to warn potential victims and thus reduce the risk of further offenses. The Supreme Court of Alaska has since held that a similar but not identical retroactive application of the statute violated the due process clause of the Alaska Constitution. Doe v. State, 92 P.3d 398 (Alaska 2004).

CHAPTER EIGHT

ANCILLARY REMEDIES

A. ENFORCING THE JUDGMENT

1. Enforcing Coercive Orders: The Contempt Power

a. The Three Kinds of Contempt

Page 786. After note 3a., add:

Does *Bagwell* require any greater procedural protections in civil contempt proceedings involving complex facts and large liabilities? A panel of the Tenth Circuit said yes, but the en banc court disagreed. Federal Trade Commission v. Kuykendall, 312 F.3d 1329 (10th Cir. 2002), *vacated*, 371 F.3d 745 (10th Cir. 2004). The district court entered a consent decree enjoining certain fraudulent telemarketing practices; those practices apparently continued unabated for five more years after the decree. The district court found defendants in contempt, found that the violations had cost consumers $39 million (apparently based on defendants' gross receipts), and ordered that amount to "be deposited into a fund administered by the Commission or its agent to be used for equitable relief, including but not limited to, consumer redress." *Id.* at 1337.

The court of appeals held that this was compensatory civil contempt. Even so, the panel held that due process required greater procedural protection than the trial court's conclusory finding of damages. The panel affirmed the finding of contempt, but remanded for a jury trial on the amount of consumer losses, with the burden on the Commission to prove those losses by clear and convincing evidence.

Perhaps the most important thing about this opinion was that it separated the due process inquiry from the categories of civil and criminal contempt. And that is precisely the point that the en banc court rejected. The en banc court rejected the requirement of jury trial. And it followed law from several circuits in holding that although the fact of civil contempt must be proved by clear and convincing evidence, the amount of recovery need be proved only by a preponderance of the evidence. Note that this is an important refinement of my brief description of the standard of proof in the third paragraph of note 3.a.

Page 799. Before note 1, add:

0.1. On remand, the trial court appointed a Nigerian-born lawyer as special master. The special master went to Nigeria, found Uchechi at a boarding school, and arranged for a phone conference with the judge and a videotape message to the parents. Uchechi said she wanted to finish school in Nigeria, she wanted to take the SAT and apply to college in the United States, she wanted her Dad out of jail, and she loved both her parents but she wanted her Dad to have custody. After a final round of emergency appeals in March 2002, her father was released on modest bail and subject to travel constraints. Uchechi returned to the United States in the fall of 2002. Margaret McHugh, *Mom Embraces Her Daughter After Long Global Custody Battle*, Newark Star-Ledger (Nov. 2, 2002). Many accounts were available online -- at least for a time -- from the New Jersey press, the father's law firm, and a Nigerian website. Among the facts revealed is that Ogechi, the daughter who died of malnutrition, suffered from a congenital intestinal disorder.

Page 802. After note 11, add:

McDougal tells her version of the story in Susan McDougal, *The Woman Who Wouldn't Talk* (Carroll & Graf 2003).

12. Investment advisor Martin A. Armstrong served seven years for contempt of an order to turn over 15 million missing dollars. Then, after a spell in solitary confinement, he plead guilty to criminal fraud. The court then found that confinement for civil contempt had lost its coercive effect, sentenced Armstrong to five years on the fraud charge, and denied credit for time served. Michael J. de la Merced, *Jailed 7 Years for Contempt, Adviser is Headed for Prison*, N.Y. Times, Apr. 28, 2007, at B4, available at 2007 WLNR 8041167. Prison officials imposed the solitary confinement after Armstrong allegedly damaged an air vent. Gretchen Morgenson,

Adviser Jailed Since 2000 Pleads Guilty in Securities Fraud Case, N.Y. Times, Aug. 18, 2006, at C5, available at 2006 WLNR 14302135. So solitary was not imposed to increase the coercive effect of the contempt sentence. But why not? Might tightening the conditions of confinement be a better solution than prolonging these standoffs for years?

There are numerous reported and unreported opinions in Armstrong's case; you can find them by keyciting Armstrong v. Guccione, 470 F.3d 89 (2d Cir. 2006). In that opinion, the court ordered the case assigned to a new judge on remand, not because the first judge had erred, but because after seven years, the "case deserves a fresh look by a different pair of eyes." *Id.* at 113. There are also some two dozen stories in the New York Times; you can find them by searching for "Martin A. Armstrong."

13. A long-running imprisonment for contempt was upheld in Chadwick v. Janecka, 312 F.3d 597 (3d Cir. 2002). Early in 1993, Beatty Chadwick transferred $2.5 million in marital assets into various offshore accounts, putting the money beyond reach of a Pennsylvania divorce court. The court ordered the money returned and held Mr. Chadwick in civil contempt when he refused. Mr. Chadwick attempted to flee the jurisdiction, but was arrested on April 5, 1995 and has been in jail since. As of 2002, he had filed eight state-court petitions and six federal-court petitions seeking release. The Pennsylvania Superior Court, in an unreported opinion, held that it was no part of the law of Pennsylvania that a contemnor must be released when he convinced the court that he would never comply. The state supreme court denied review.

Mr. Chadwick then filed a federal habeas corpus proceeding. The federal district court ordered him released, but stayed the order pending appeal. 2002 WL 12292 (E.D. Pa. 2002). The named defendant, Janecka, runs the county jail where Mr. Chadwick is held. Janecka did not appeal, but Mrs. Chadwick intervened and appealed, and the court of appeals upheld her standing to do so.

Federal review on habeas is limited; the standard is whether the state court's decision was "contrary to, or involved an unreasonable application of, clearly established Federal law, as determined by the Supreme Court of the United States." 28 U.S.C. §2254(d) (2000). In context, this can only mean federal constitutional law; the federal law of civil contempt would not be binding on Pennsylvania, although the opinion does not seem to make that distinction. The Third Circuit relies on a sentence in *Bagwell* stating that the "paradigmatic" civil contempt sanction "involves confining a contemnor indefinitely until he complies." This is obviously dictum; no issue of perpetual coercion was before the Court in *Bagwell*. But the dictum seemed to speak quite clearly. The Third Circuit showed convincingly that *Maggio* was about inability to comply, not unwillingness to comply. With no Supreme Court case suggesting unwillingness to comply as a limit on coercion, there was no basis to interfere with the decision of the Pennsylvania courts. Beyond that, the Third Circuit treated it as an open question whether the dictum in *Bagwell* implicitly overruled lower federal court cases releasing contemnors after coercion had failed.

The courts have since denied a ninth state habeas petition. Chadwick v. Caulfield, 834 A.2d 562 (Pa. Super. 2003), *appeal denied*, 853 A.2d 359 (Pa. 2004), *cert. denied*, 543 U.S. 875 (2004). Further appeals continue to be denied in summary orders without reported opinions. Chadwick v. Chadwick, 916 A.2d 630 (Pa. 2007); Chadwick v. Chadwick, 902 A.2d 1238 (Pa. 2006) Chadwick v. Chadwick, 879 A.2d 781 (Pa. 2005). The state supreme court also suspended Chadwick's law license for five years. Office of Disciplinary Counsel v. Chadwick, 874 A.2d 1142 (Pa. 2005).

Chadwick now claims that the money is irretrievably gone, but the trial court found his testimony incredible and unworthy of belief. Chadwick v. Chadwick, 68 Pa. D. & C.4th 369, 2004 WL 3092489 (Pa. Com. Pl. 2004). The court noted that Chadwick seemed to be able reach the money to pay substantial legal bills, and he had been able to reach it to purchase three annuities. The court found the wife's unpaid share of the missing property to be $2.8 million, and awarded an additional $1.4 million in attorneys' fees. The court appointed "forensic accountants" and a retired state judge to trace the money; the Associated Press reports that they found nothing. Erin McClam, *Bizarre Divorce Saga: A Man, a Woman and Missing Millions* (AP Sept. 17, 2006), available on Westlaw. (There appears to be no document number; search for it by author and title in the newsplus database.)

The retired judge is quoted as saying that if he had just stolen $2 million dollars, he would have done his time and been out by now. Mr. Chadwick's lawyer says that if they want to find the money, they should let him out of jail and follow him. "Nothing else has worked." Nicole Weisensee Egan, *H. Beatty Chadwick Would Rather Do Jail Time -- A Dozen Years and Counting -- Than Settle with His Ex*, People Magazine, May 14, 2007, available at 2007 WLNR 8479647.

Chadwick has been in jail for twelve years now; the press claims that this is the longest time served for coercive civil contempt in American history. The AP story attributes the previous record of ten years to Odell Sheppard, a Chicago father whose daughter had disappeared. He claimed to know nothing of her whereabouts; the court thought he knew and wouldn't talk. He was released in 1998 when the girl's mother died.

Daisy Tegtmeyer, a family trustee who refused to distribute assets or answer questions about the trust, did at least nine years from 1933 to 1942. The press doesn't know about this one, and the reported opinions do not reveal when she was released, but the last reported opinion suggests that soon, her testimony would no longer be needed. Tegtmeyer v. Tegtmeyer, 40 N.E.2d 767 (Ill App. 1942); Tegtmeyer v. Tegtmeyer, 28 N.E.2d 303 (Ill. App. 1940); Tegtmeyer v. Tegtmeyer, 11 N.E. 2d 657 (Ill. App. 1937).

14. The press apparently accepts "freelance videographer" Josh Wolf as the journalist imprisoned the longest for withholding information. Jessie McKinley, *Jail Record Near for Videographer Who Resisted Grand Jury*, N.Y. Times A15 (Feb. 6, 2007), available at 2007 WLNR 2244034. The government denied that Wolf was a journalist, but that issue was never resolved. Wolf published on his blog video of a demonstration that turned violent; the government demanded that he produce the original of the video and testify to the grand jury. The order affirming the finding of contempt is In re Grand Jury Subpoena, 201 Fed. Appx. 430 (9th Cir. 2006). Wolf was released after seven and a half months when he agreed to turn over the raw footage and the government agreed not to seek his testimony; the deal was reached through court-supervised mediation. Bob Egelko & Jim Herron Zamora, *The Josh Wolf Case: Blogger*

Freed After Giving Video to Feds, San Francisco Chronicle B1 (April 4, 2007), available at 2007 WLNR 6415950.

Page 811. After note 8, add:

9. The fiftieth anniversary of Brown v. Board of Education brought a long retrospective on the school closing in Prince Edward County. June Kronholz, *Education Gap - After 45 Years, A School Lockout Still Reverberates*, Wall St. J. A1 (May 17, 2004). The county was rural and somewhat poor when the schools closed in 1959, and it is rural and somewhat poor today. Statistical comparisons are inconclusive, but one is suggestive: in 1960, the average wage was 55% higher in Prince Edward than in neighboring Cumberland County; today, the average wage in the two counties is about the same. Prince Edward has a whole set of middle-aged adults -- mostly black, but also some whites whose parents could not afford the private school -- who still suffer from losing so much education. Some of the older kids did not return when the schools reopened; younger kids were skipped over several grades, and some of them can barely read or write. The schools were closed for five years; my confident claim of nine was apparently a deeply rooted trick of memory. If I had not been so sure, I would have checked.

Today, the county has one school for each grade level, and it is integrated. The population is 62% white, but the elected sheriff is black and there are blacks on the city council and county board.

2. Collecting Money Judgments

a. Execution, Garnishment, and the Like

Page 860. After note 9, add:

10. Students take warning: The United States can collect your student loans by withholding your social security benefits -- and there is no statute of limitations! Lockhart v. United States, 546 U.S. 142 (2005). In a wide range of circumstances where parties owe each other offsetting debts, the side that is not being paid may decide to "set off" (that is, net out) the offsetting debts. If you have a loan

from your bank and a deposit at your bank, the bank can set off the deposit and apply it to the loan. Less likely, if the bank fails and your deposit exceeds the limits on deposit insurance, you can set off your loan against your lost deposit. The government can generally collect debts by set off, but social security benefits are generally exempt from any form of collection, including set off by the government. But student loans are an exception to the exemption of social security benefits, and student loans are also an exception to the general ten-year statute of limitations on collection of debts owing the federal government. The Supreme Court had to sort out the interaction of four statutes that create these rules, but the Congressional intent seems clear enough and the result is now settled.

11. The en banc Fifth Circuit has sanctioned a lawyer for using a writ of execution to embarrass the judgment debtor and promote himself. Whitehead v. Food Max, Inc., 332 F.3d 796 (5th Cir. 2003). Three days after the court denied defendant K-Mart's motion for new trial, the lawyer arrived at a K-Mart with a writ of execution and local TV crews, demanding all the cash on hand. K-Mart claimed it was protected from execution for ten days, giving it time to further delay execution by filing a bond; that dispute was never resolved.

Assuming that K-Mart was subject to execution when the writ was executed, the court sanctioned the attorney for using the writ for improper purposes. There was no prospect of collecting a significant portion of the $3.4 million judgment from the cash in one store; plaintiff had a lien on all K-Mart's real property in the state; and these events occurred in 1997, well before any known risk that K-Mart might be sliding into bankruptcy. The court concluded that the execution was not for legitimate purposes of collection, but for illegitimate purposes related to the publicity it would generate.

Page 862. After note 3, add:

3.1. The federal Bankruptcy Code contains a set of federal exemptions, 11 U.S.C. §522 (2000 & Supp.), that apply in bankruptcy court unless the debtor's state has opted out, in which case that state's exemptions apply. This federal provision exempts payments under "a stock bonus, pension, profitsharing, annuity, or similar plan or contract on account of illness, disability, death, age, or length of service, to the extent reasonably necessary for the support of the debtor and any dependent," with a narrow exception aimed at abuses by corporate insiders. 11 U.S.C. §522(d)(10(E). Resolving a persistent circuit split, the Supreme Court has held that Individual Retirement Accounts (IRAs) are within this exemption. Rousey v. Jacoway, 544 U.S. 320 (2005). Some lower courts had held that IRAs are not exempt, because unlike an employer-sponsored pension plan, they can be cashed in at any time if the owner is willing to pay the tax penalties. The Supreme Court disagreed, holding that the tax penalties were a substantial deterrent to cashing in, and that the actual rate of early withdrawals is quite low.

Note the limitation to amounts "reasonably necessary for the support of the debtor and any dependent." This contrasts sharply with the unlimited exemption in the Texas statute. But how is a judge supposed to decide how much is "reasonably necessary"? Congress might have provided a presumptive number, rebuttable on a showing of special circumstances such as disability or unusual medical bills. But that might have required more consensus than Congress could muster.

The Bankruptcy Abuse Prevention and Consumer Protection Act of 2005 makes a start. The act made extensive amendments to the Bankruptcy Code, including to §522. The exemption at issue in *Rousey* -- exempt *payments* from retirement plans -- is unchanged. Congress has added an exemption for *accumulations* in retirement plans. This exemption is available whether debtor elects the state or federal exemptions; it appears in §522(b)(3)(C) and again in §§522(d)(12) and 522(n). The new exemption avoids ambiguity by listing specific sections of the Internal Revenue Code; any plan under one of those sections is exempt. IRAs and Roth IRAs are included; the accumulations in most employer-managed plans would not be part of the bankruptcy estate in any event. For the covered plans, the exemption is presumptively capped at $1 million. It may sound absurd to let a person keep $1 million while discharging all his debts; certainly most Americans do not retire with $1 million stashed away. But the mandatory distribution at age 70 from a million-dollar IRA is only a little over $36,000, which may not seem so lavish. Of course there may be other retirement plans or pensions, and there will be social security benefits; a more sensible limit would take account of the total picture instead of singling out IRAs for special treatment. But again, that would have required too much consensus.

3.2. The act also puts new limits on homestead exemptions. Bowie Kuhn, the former Commissioner of Baseball, moved to Florida before filing for bankruptcy, to take advantage of the unlimited homestead exemption there. To prevent such abuses, the act requires a debtor to have lived in a state for 730 days before filing for bankruptcy to claim the state exemptions. §522(b)(3)(A). If the debtor has moved in that time, he gets the exemptions from the state where he lived for the largest part of the 180 days preceding the 730 day period -- that is, from where he lived two years before filing.

Other provisions are aimed at debtors who pour liquid assets into an exempt homestead -- by buying a bigger house or paying down the mortgage -- before filing for bankruptcy. Empirical studies show that there are few such people, but we know there are some. The debtor cannot claim as exempt more than $125,000 of home equity acquired in the 1,215 days (39 months) before filing. §522(p). And if at any time in the preceding ten years he sold nonexempt assets and invested that money in his house, with intent to hinder or defraud any creditor, he cannot retain the equity so acquired. §522(o).

Page 868. After note 5, add:

5.1. New York has simplified the process, with dramatic results. The judgment creditor can serve "an information subpoena" on any person, posing written questions to be answered by return mail. N.Y. C.P.L.R. §5224(a)3. (Supp. 2007). The key change is that, if the target of the subpoena agrees, the questions can be submitted electronically. §5224(a)4. This has made it possible for collection agencies to send electronic lists of all their judgment debtors to every bank in New York, asking each bank to electronically compare the list to its list of depositors. The practice, and its results, are described in Lucette Lagnado, *Cold-Case Files: Dunned for Old*

Bills, Poor Find Some Hospitals Never Forget, Wall St. J. A1 (June 8, 2004).

When a bank reports a match, the "attorney for the judgment creditor as officer of the court" serves a restraining notice under §5222(a). The notice freezes the account, up to twice the amount that the notice states is due, for a year. §5222(b). The notice can also be served electronically. §5222(g). Once it serves a restraining notice, the creditor must send the judgment debtor a written notice explaining that he might be able to get his money back if it came from an exempt source, unless such a notice has been sent within the preceding year. §5222(d) and (e).

The procedure is so cheap that it makes it worthwhile to troll repeatedly for debtors on old judgments. As the *Journal* story summarizes: "Collectors in New York once had to laboriously track down each delinquent debtor's branch bank, asking one bank after another in the debtor's neighborhood to search its files. . . . [but now] 'it is basically a blitz -- you blitz all the banks,'" quoting the director of a collection agency. Judgments should not go unpaid because of the expense of collection procedures; more efficient procedures are surely to be desired. Agencies collecting child support can troll for bank accounts as easily as agencies collecting credit card debt.

But the New York practice is much more efficient at identifying assets than at protecting exemptions. Ninety percent of earnings are exempt in New York, unless not reasonably needed for the support of the debtor and his dependents. §5205(d). But the exemption is apparently good only if the creditor garnishes the earnings at the source, *see id.* (defining the exempt wages in terms of the date of an income execution), and perhaps in bankruptcy for funds still identifiable as recent earnings, In re Wrobel, 268 B.R. 342 (Bankr. W.D.N.Y. 2001). Surely most of the money in small bank accounts is from earnings, so the new procedure efficiently bypasses the exemption; wage earners without savings are left with no funds to pay rent or buy groceries.

5.2. A federal court has held that New Jersey would recognize a tort of "creditor fraud," which may be committed by third parties who assist the debtor in concealing assets. Morganroth & Morganroth v. Norris, McLaughlin & Marcus, P.C., 331 F.3d 406 (3d Cir. 2003). As the name of the case hints, the defendant here was the law firm that represented the debtor. The tort does not require false representations directly to the creditors, nor does it require that the creditors rely on any false representations. The allegations in *Morganroth* were that the defendant law firm actively planned and participated in the creation of sham transactions to conceal assets, drafted documents for those sham transactions, and in general, "went beyond the bounds of permissible advocacy." *Id.* at 412.

The debtor in this case is John DeLorean, famous in the early 1980s for manufacturing a distinctive stainless-steel luxury car, the DeLorean. The company failed, and only 8,000 cars were ever built, but their owners remain loyal. The plaintiff in *Morganroth* was his Michigan law firm, which claims to have done $6 million worth of work over ten years without being paid -- obviously not a prudent way to practice law.

5.3. New Jersey has rejected *Morganroth* and refused to recognize a tort of creditor fraud. Banco Popular North America v. Gandi, 876 A.2d 253 (N.J. 2005). It held instead that there is a more specific and better defined tort -- civil conspiracy to violate the fraudulent transfer laws. These laws are summarized in the main volume at pages 689-690. An attorney and his client can conspire to violate these laws; in *Banco Popular*, the attorney advised the client to transfer all his assets to his wife, and the client acted on that advice. The court also held that the creditor could *not* sue the attorney for negligent misrepresentation in the course of the fraudulent transfer, but could sue for negligent misrepresentation in loan negotiations and in an opinion letter issued in connection with the loan negotiations. A law license is not a license to do just anything on behalf of a client; there are limits to the adversary system.

Page 887. After note 8, add:

8.1. Note 8 got a little too terse, and it had a critical typo. A crime victim's claim for damages is in principle *dis*chargeable, not nondischargeable, but there are, as noted, a patchwork of exceptions covering a wide range of crimes.

Section 523(a)(13) makes nondischargeable any order entered under title 18 of United States Code, the federal criminal code.

Section 523(a)(7) makes nondischargeable a "fine, penalty, or forfeiture," payable "to and for the benefit of a governmental unit," that "is not compensation for actual pecuniary loss." So restitution to the crime victim would seem to be plainly precluded as not "for the benefit of a governmental unit," and doubly precluded if it is equal to the amount of the victim's "actual pecuniary loss." No problem according to In re Thompson, 418 F.3d 362 (3d Cir. 2005), which says that federalism concerns about federal interference with state criminal proceedings trump statutory text. *Thompson* distinguishes In re Towers on the ground that in *Towers*, Illinois had obtained a restitution order for victims in a civil proceeding, not a criminal proceeding, so federalism concerns were much weaker.

B. LITIGATION EXPENSES

Page 912. After note 4, add:

4.1. Sometimes the Court says the right to file a lawsuit is constitutionally protected, part of the First Amendment right to petition the government for redress of grievances. These cases are a limit on doctrines that occasionally treat meritless lawsuits filed to harass as unfair labor practices or violations of the antitrust laws. A recent labor law example is BE & K Construction Co. v. NLRB, 536 U.S. 516 (2002). The labor board had found a violation and awarded attorneys' fees where an employer had filed an unsuccessful suit against a union for the purpose of retaliating against that union. The Court held that lack of success and retaliatory motive were not enough; the board must also find that there was no reasonable basis for the lawsuit. After much talk about the First Amendment, the court interpreted the National Labor Relations Act not to authorize liability.

This would seem to suggest a constitutional right to file weak lawsuits and not suffer fee awards, except for lawsuits lacking any reasonable basis. But the Court denied that implication: "[N]othing in our opinion today should be read to question the validity of common litigation sanctions imposed by courts themselves . . . or the validity of statutory provisions that merely authorize the imposition of attorney's fees on a losing plaintiff." Justice Scalia, concurring, explained that First Amendment rights are more threatened when an executive branch agency awards fees than when an Article III court awards the same fees; the principal difference he relied on was the guarantee of judicial independence.

Page 914. After note 2, add:

2.1. An illustration with great facts is In re the Marriage of Powell, 170 S.W.3d 156 (Tex. App.--Eastland 2005). Husband, ordered to pay $1,000 in fees to wife's attorney, arrived at the attorney's office with 20 bags of unrolled pennies. He testified that he did it "to make a hardship upon him." The attorney bizarrely testified that it took him 2.7496 hours to collect and redeem the pennies. (That number does not appear to have resulted from converting a sensible fraction to decimals; I calculate it at 2 hours, 44 minutes, 58.56 seconds.) The court held husband not in contempt, but finding his conduct "frivolous and ridiculous," ordered him to pay attorneys' fees for the time spent picking up pennies, plus the $100 bank charge for redeeming the pennies, plus $83 in court costs.

Page 915. After note 10, add:

11. If you have a valid claim for attorneys' fees, and your defendant goes bankrupt, can you claim the attorneys' fees in the bankruptcy proceeding? Well, yes but maybe not, according to the Supreme Court. The Court unanimously rejected a Ninth Circuit rule that fees may not be awarded to creditors for litigating bankruptcy issues. Travelers Casualty & Surety Co. v. Pacific Gas & Electric Co., 127 S.Ct. 1199 (2007). That rule was a judicial policy judgment with no basis in the text of the Bankruptcy Code. The debtor tried to defend the judgment on the alternate ground that 11 U.S.C. §506(b) (Supp. 2006), which allows "any reasonable fees, costs, or charges provided for under the agreement or State statute under which such claim arose," allows these "fees" etc. only to secured creditors and only to the extent that their collateral covers the claim. By implication, the argument is, unsecured creditors can never recover attorneys' fees. The Court declined to resolve this issue, because it had not been considered below or presented in the brief in

opposition to certiorari. The case involved a contractual claim to attorneys' fees, but the reasoning of the Court and of the parties (on both issues) seems equally applicable to any other claim for attorneys' fees.

Page 919. After note 7, add:

8. Another statute providing that courts "may" award fees is the removal statute. Federal jurisdiction is usually permissive rather than exclusive; for cases that could be filed in federal court, plaintiffs usually have a choice of filing either in state or federal court. When plaintiff chooses state court, defendants often have the option to "remove" to federal court cases that could have been filed there in the first place. 28 U.S.C. §§1441-1447 (2000 & Supp.). If defendant removes a case to federal court and the federal court determines that it lacks jurisdiction, it must "remand" the case to state court. And when the federal court remands a case to state court, it "may" award the costs and attorneys' fees "incurred as a result of the removal." 28 U.S.C. §1447(c) (2000).

In Martin v. Franklin Capital Corp., 546 U.S. 132 (2006), the Court held that fees should generally be awarded only if "the removing party lacked an objectively reasonable basis for seeking removal." *Id.* at 141. District courts also "retain discretion to consider . . . unusual circumstances," such as "a plaintiff's delay in seeking remand or [plaintiff's] failure to disclose facts necessary to determine jurisdiction." *Id.* In *Martin*, the removal petition was based on precedents later rejected in the relevant circuit, so defendant clearly had an objectively reasonable basis for removal at the time it attempted to remove.

Martin reviews, with apparent approval, the civil rights cases creating a strong presumption in favor of one-way fee shifting. And it succinctly states the longstanding but often implicit presumption that one who brings unsuccessful litigation has not done anything wrong. Speaking of the defendant who unsuccessfully seeks to remove, the Court says that "incorrectly invoking a federal right is not comparable to violating substantive federal law." *Id.* at 137.

143

Page 920. After note 2, add:

A good illustration is Mercer v. Duke University, 401 F.3d 199 (4th Cir. 2005). Heather Mercer was a place kicker who made the Duke football team as a walk-on in 1995, generating widespread publicity. Fearing that the publicity would hurt recruiting, the coach changed his mind; thereafter, he refused to let her suit up, repeatedly insulted her, and eventually cut her from the team. She sued under Title IX of the Education Amendments of 1972, 20 U.S.C. §1681 *et seq.* (2000), which prohibits sex discrimination in federally assisted educational institutions. An exception provides that women need not be allowed to participate in single-sex contact sports, but the court held that this exception did not permit discrimination against women who were allowed to participate. A jury awarded $1 in nominal damages and $800,000 in punitive damages, but the punitives were thrown out under Barnes v. Gorman, described in the supplement to pages 734 and 1051, which held that punitives are not available under Title IX.

Even so, the court upheld an award of $350,000 in attorneys' fees. Plaintiff had recovered only a small fraction of the relief she sought, but she had established an important legal principle and served the public interest. Other women were following in her footsteps -- a handful in colleges and nearly 3,000 in high schools -- and her precedent would be available to them.

Page 920. After note 5, add:

6. Fee awards, and ordinary contingent fees, gave rise to a long running tax issue that has at last been mostly resolved. Except for personal injury awards exempt from tax under 26 U.S.C. §104 (2000) (see Norfolk & Western Ry. v. Liepelt at page 201 of the main volume), a monetary recovery is generally taxable income to the plaintiff. Attorneys' fees are a cost of producing that income, and thus generally deductible, but attorneys fees were not deductible in calculating the alternative minimum tax. A large spike in income with a correspondingly large deduction often threw successful plaintiffs into the alternative minimum tax. So a plaintiff who recovered $100,000 and paid $40,000 to his attorney often owed tax

on the full $100,000, without any usable deduction for the fees. Cases like *Riverside* were far worse; plaintiffs who recovered only $33,000 in damages might owe tax on a total recovery of $278,000, most of which went to their attorneys. With damages of $33,000 and taxes in excess of $70,000, successful plaintiffs in such cases faced financial ruin. And of course, the fees are taxed again when the attorney receives them as income.

Successful plaintiffs tried to escape the tax liability by arguing that the fees went directly from defendant to their attorney. In Commissioner v. Banks, 543 U.S. 426 (2005), the Supreme Court rejected that argument, at least for ordinary contingent fees. Defendant owes the amount of the judgment to plaintiff; plaintiff owes fees to the attorney. The fees are taxable at each step of the transaction, and plaintiff cannot avoid tax by assigning the fees to his attorney. The Court did not reach the question of statutory fee awards; the same reasoning would seem to apply, but the affront to common sense would be considerably greater, and plaintiffs argued that the policy of the fee award statute should modify or override the policy of the Internal Revenue Code.

Congress largely fixed the problem for the future, in 26 U.S.C. §§62(a)(19) and 62(e) (Supp IV. 2004), which makes many attorneys' fees deductible in calculating adjusted gross income, and thus in calculating the alternative minimum tax. The provision is not retroactive, and it applies only to a lengthy list of causes of action, mostly involving claims by employees. The problem is still there for causes of action not listed, most obviously including the environmental laws. There a tax-exempt organization can be the plaintiff; certainly no individual can afford to sue for an injunction and attorneys' fees.

Page 921. After note 4, add:

One court has held that an enforceable settlement agreement changes the legal relationship between the parties and will support a fee award, and that *Buckhannon*'s apparent requirement of a consent decree is mere dictum. Barrios v. California Interscholastic Federation, 277 F.3d 1128, 1134 & n.5 (9th Cir. 2002). The more common view appears to be that this is not enough, but that it is enough if the court retains jurisdiction to enforce the settlement agreement. Roberson v. Giuliani, 346 F.3d 75 (2d Cir. 2003). The distinction is between enforceable judicial decrees and simple contracts between the parties, elaborated in the main volume at pages 808-809. But *Buckhannon's* absurd consequences seem to be pushing courts to develop a previously murky in-between category:

> In the case of both consent decrees and private settlement agreements over which a district court retains enforcement jurisdiction, the district court has the authority to force compliance with the terms agreed upon by the parties. In the later instance, the court at most would need to take an extra step by first ordering specific performance and then, if a party does not comply, finding that party in contempt. We doubt that the definition of "prevailing party" should turn on such a difference.

Roberson, 346 F.3d at 83.

5. An attempt to study *Buckhanon's* effects empirically is reported in Catherine R. Albiston & Laura Beth Nielsen, *The Procedural Attack on Civil Rights: The Empirical Reality of Buckhannon for the Private Attorney General*, http://ssrn.com/abstract=937114, forthcoming in 54 UCLA L. Rev. ---- (June 2007). They offer examples of "strategic capitulation," in which defendants litigate until they face an imminent risk of adverse judgment and then surrender, avoiding fee liability. SSRN manuscript at 17-29. The empirical part of the study is a survey of public interest organizations, asking if they had been adversely affected by *Buckhannon*. This is not terribly satisfactory; they did not ask these organizations to support their conclusions with data or examples. Many organizations in the sample had never received a fee award even before *Buckhannon*; of course they had not been adversely affected. So it is hard to make much of the data. But those organizations most likely to say they were negatively affected were the ones the authors predicted: organizations that filed class actions, engaged in impact litigation, were negatively affected by the growth of sovereign immunity, and/or engaged in environmental, poverty, or civil rights law. *Id.* at 34-39. But politically conservative litigating

organizations were as likely as liberal organizations to report negative effects. *Id.* at 43.

The authors also asked for explanations or comments on *Buckhannon*'s effects. *Id.* at 39-42. They got reports of strategic capitulation. They were also told that cases are harder to settle, because defendant can no longer settle without admitting liability. Defendant must submit to a judgment or plaintiff forfeits his fees. It is harder to get private attorneys to take cases, or to assist with cases, because they are less likely to recover fees. Case selection is affected, sometimes in surprising ways. As a lawyer reported in a different article, "If a case comes in the door and it's so good that the defense is likely to cave before it ever gets to trial, we can't afford to take that case because we're never going to get paid when it settles." Attorney Donald Feldman, quoted in Margaret Graham Tebo, *Fee-Shifting Fallout*, ABA Journal 54, 57 (July 2003).

6. What if a preliminary injunction accomplishes one of plaintiff's principal purposes in the lawsuit, and the case ultimately becomes moot, in part because of the beneficial effects of the preliminary injunction? Several circuits have held that this can make the plaintiff a prevailing party, because plaintiff's benefits from the preliminary injunction are a court-ordered change in the relationship between the parties. The Fourth Circuit disagrees. Some of the cases are collected in Select Milk Producers, Inc. v. Johanns, 400 F.3d 939 (D.C. Cir. 2005).

The Supreme Court reserved that issue in Sole v. Wyner, 127 S.Ct. 2188 (2007), where plaintiff got a preliminary injunction (permitting a nude peace demonstration on a Florida beach), but later lost the case in a final judgment upholding Florida's "Bathing Suit Rule" and refusing to enjoin the rule's enforcement against any further nude demonstrations. The Court unanimously held that plaintiffs were not a prevailing party. Their initial success was "ephemeral," *id.* at 2196, and it was "superseded" by the final judgment, *id.* at 2195-96.

7. At least three circuits have held *Buckhannon* inapplicable to fee awards under the Clean Air Act, 42 U.S.C. §7607(f) (2000), which authorizes fees "whenever [the court] determines such award is appropriate." There is no express prevailing-party requirement. The Supreme Court has held that fee awards to a losing party are

never appropriate, Ruckelshaus v. Sierra Club, 463 U.S. 680 (1983), but a dictum in that case cited legislative history that it would be appropriate to award fees to a plaintiff whose lawsuit induced defendant to comply prior to judgment. *Id.* at 686 n.8. *Buckhannon* does not cite *Ruckelshaus*, and the emerging view is that the *Ruckelshaus* footnote survives. Sierra Club v. Environmental Protection Agency, 322 F.3d 718 (D.C. Cir. 2003).

7. The California court has squarely rejected *Buckhannon* as a matter of state law. Plaintiffs seeking fees under California statutes may recover on a catalyst theory if the underlying litigation had merit and plaintiff made a reasonable attempt to settle the dispute prior to filing suit. Graham v. DaimlerChrysler Corp., 101 P.3d 140 (Cal. 2005).

Page 921. Before note 1, add:

0.1. I have always thought that "lodestar" was an unfortunate term. It reminds me of "the mother lode" and attorneys pursuing great quantities of gold. In fact, "lodestar" refers to a leading or guiding star, and the "lode" in lodestar comes from a completely different Middle English word than the "lode" that means a vein of ore. But I may not be the only one to confuse the two words.

I mention this now because a panel of the Second Circuit has abandoned the word "lodestar." Arbor Hill Concerned Citizens Neighborhood Association v. County of Albany, 484 F.3d 162 (2d Cir. 2007). The panel thought that the Supreme Court had tried to combine the lodestar method with the twelve *Johnson* factors (see footnote 3 at page 906 of the main volume) without ever explaining the relationship between the two. I would have said -- I think I still would say -- that the *Johnson* factors were mere window dressing, doing no work but retained because of their prominence in legislative history. But the court in *Arbor Hill* thought they were modifying the lodestar in ways that made it no longer much of a guiding star. The court proposed a new formulation: that the "reasonable hourly rate is the rate a paying client would be willing to pay." *Id.* at 169. And in determining that rate, the court should consider that the client might be able to negotiate a reduced rate because of the attorneys' "desire to obtain the reputational benefits that might accrue from being associated with the case." *Id.* Is this any different from the rejected idea of paying below-market rates to altruistic public interest lawyers?

The court did not purport to bind future panels of the Second Circuit to avoid the word "lodestar." "[I]t is too well entrenched," but "this panel believes that it is a term whose time has come." *Id.* n.2. The opinion may get more attention because of the composition of the panel: Judge Walker (writing), Chief Judge Jacobs, and Justice O'Connor, sitting by designation.

Page 930. Before note 1, add:

0.1. From the $46 million awarded to the insurer class, the trial judge on remand awarded 22%, plus expenses, to the insurers' lawyers. These fees were based on the average of the insurers' fee agreements with their lawyers. 201 F. Supp. 2d 861 (N.D. Ill. 2002). The court of appeals affirmed. 325 F.3d 974, 976-977 (7th Cir. 2003).

From the $88 million awarded to the consumer class, the trial judge awarded 30% of the first $10 million, 25% of the second $10 million, 20% of the third $10 million, 15% of the fourth $10 million, and 10% of the remaining $48 million, an average of 15%, with no separate award for expenses. These percentages were based in part on the outcome of fee auctions in securities fraud cases.

The court of appeals reversed again. The lawyers for the consumer class had developed the case and taken most of the risk; the lawyers for the insurer class had piggybacked on their efforts. Because the consumer lawyers had borne more risk, they should also get more pay. But in the range from $20 to $45 million, the insurer lawyers got a larger fraction of their recovery than the consumer lawyers got of theirs. The court rejected the analogy to the auctions in securities cases, partly because of problems it thought were inherent in fee auctions, and partly because there was no evidence comparing the risk in securities cases to the risk in this case.

Frustrated with the delay of two appeals and with the district judge, the court of appeals made its own fee award, modifying the district court's structure as little as it thought possible. It awarded 22% of the recovery between $20 million and $45 million, on the theory that the consumer lawyers bore at least as much risk as the insurer lawyers in that range, and 15% of the excess over $46 million, raising the average to nearly 20%. And it ordered a separate award of expenses on remand. *Id.* at 977-980.

Page 938. After note 11, add:

11.1. In re Cavanaugh, 306 F.3d 726 (9th Cir. 2002), reads the Securities Reform Act to preclude consideration of the fee agreement in appointment of lead counsel, except where the agreement is so unreasonable that it casts doubt on plaintiff's adequacy as a class representative. The trial court had appointed the plaintiff with the second largest claim, on the ground that he had negotiated much lower attorneys' fees -- 10 to 15 percent of any recovery, with the percentage declining as the recovery grew, and with a cap of $8 million. The plaintiffs with the largest claim had hired Milberg Weiss, perhaps the nation's most prominent class-action law firm, and agreed to fees where the percentage increased to 30% as the recovery grew, with no cap. The court of appeals was not surprised that the more established firm charged more than the less established firm. More fundamentally, it gave strong effect to the statutory presumption in favor of the plaintiff with the largest claim, and suggested that the time to police fee awards would come when plaintiffs and their counsel sought approval of the award. All of this was decided before trial, on a petition for mandamus.

On remand, Milberg Weiss and the plaintiffs with the largest claim failed to appear despite repeated notices. The plaintiff whose claim had been second largest now had the largest claim of any plaintiffs still seeking appointment as lead counsel, and the district court again appointed that plaintiff. In re Copper Mountain Securities Litigation, 305 F. Supp. 2d 1124 (N.D. Cal. 2004). There is a wonderful opinion about how Prince Charming sometimes vanquishes the villain and rescues the princess, and sometimes turns out to be a frog. The trial judge suggests that perhaps Milberg Weiss was mainly interested in the precedent it established in *Cavanaugh* -- it can be appointed no matter how high its fees if it collects the largest group of plaintiffs -- and not really interested in the *Copper Mountain* litigation.

Recent amendments to Rule 23, on class actions, require the court to consider various factors going to the ability of counsel seeking to represent the class. "If more than one adequate applicant seeks appointment as class counsel, the court must appoint the applicant best able to represent the interests of the class." "The order appointing class counsel may include provisions about the award of attorney fees." All these provisions appear in Fed. R. Civ. Proc. 23(g). This is obviously a very different approach from *Cavanaugh*'s. The Securities Reform Act requires the lead plaintiff to satisfy "the requirements of Rule 23." 15 U.S.C. §77z-1(a)(3)(B)(iii)(I)(cc) (2000). Is Rule 23(g) such a requirement? Or is it an alternate set of instructions for how to appoint class counsel, effective only in cases where the Securities Reform Act does not apply?

Page 939. After note 15, add:

16. The Supreme Court got a small-scale version of this debate in Gisbrecht v. Barnhart, 535 U.S. 789 (2002). In suits to collect back benefits under the Social Security Act, the Act authorizes "a reasonable fee . . . not in excess of 25% of the . . . past-due benefits." 42 U.S.C. §406(b)(1)(A) (2000). The fee is set by the court as part of the judgment, but paid by the client out of the benefits awarded, and it is a criminal offense for a lawyer to charge more. The question was what the limitation to "a reasonable fee" adds to the 25% cap.

The district court had interpreted "reasonable" to mean the lodestar, and awarded hourly fees ranging from $3,000 to $6,000, which were 11 to 18 percent of the amount recovered. The Court reversed, convincingly showing that Congress had not meant to require hourly fees. The Court emphasized that "the lodestar method was designed to govern imposition of fees on the losing party." 535 U.S. at 806.

It held that courts should look "first to the contingent-fee agreement," but the evidence was that attorneys uniformly contract for the 25% maximum. Then the court should test that agreement for reasonableness. The agreement might be unreasonable if the lawyer's delay had increased the amount of back benefits (because more benefits accrue each month), or "if the benefits are large in comparison to the amount of time counsel spent on the case." *Id.* at 808. The court may require time records, "not as a basis for satellite litigation, but as an aid to the court's assessment of the reasonableness of the fee yielded by the fee agreement." *Id.* This sounds a lot like the Second and Third Circuit's approach and the district court's first opinion in *Synthroid.*

Only Justice Scalia dissented. He thought the reasonableness of a contingent fee could be assessed before the case began, but not after the results were known. For after-the-fact fee setting, the Court had held that the lodestar is the only measure of reasonableness, and the lodestar should be applied here. He ridiculed the majority's approach as standardless.

Page 940. After note 3, add:

4. The Individuals with Disabilities Education Act, which guarantees an individualized education plan to all disabled children, authorizes an award to prevailing parents of "reasonable attorneys' fees as part of the costs." 20 U.S.C. 1415(i)(3)(B) (2000). The Court has held that this does not include expert witness fees. Arlington Central School District Board of Education v. Murphy, 126 S.Ct. 2455 (2006). This would be a routine application of *Crawford Fitting* and *Casey*, except that the Conference Report approved by both the House and Senate said expressly and unambiguously that expert witness fees were to be included, and the statute itself directed a study of the "fees, costs, and expenses" awarded to prevailing parties and of the hours spent by "attorneys and consultants." But the IDEA is a Spending Clause legislation; states must comply with its terms only if they accept federal money to help carry it out, and states are entitled to clear notice of the rules that attach when they accept the money. Justice Alito for the majority said that neither legislative history nor the study provision could provide such notice when the text of the fee-award provision used language that had been construed not to include expert witness fees. Three dissenters thought the scope of fee awards was the sort of detail to which the clear notice requirement does not apply, and that Congressional intent was unambiguous.

Page 952. After note 5, add:

5.1. Various bar association ethics committees have disapproved fee agreements providing that if the client rejects the lawyer's settlement advice, the fee changes from contingent fee to an hourly rate. Some of these opinions are collected in Opinion 2001-1 of the Philadelphia Bar Association's Professional Guidance Committee, available at *www.philabar.org.* (Click on Publications and Resources, then Ethics Opinions; then they are organized by date.) But the Philadelphia committee said that such an agreement could be valid if the goals of the representation were set out in the agreement. The idea seems to be that if the client agrees to accept a settlement offer of X, and to pay extra fees if he rejects an offer of X, he can be held to that agreement when he changes his mind. Of course it can be extraordinarily difficult to determine a reasonable X at the inception of the attorney-client relationship, when the attorney knows little about the case. X might have to be defined in terms of a range, or elements of harm. And all of this was in the context of clients paying their own lawyers, although it is hard to see why attorney-client agreements concerning a potential fee award should be different.

5.2. One place where fee waivers may have become universal is Los Angeles County. See Bernhardt v. Los Angeles County, 339 F.3d 920 (9th Cir. 2003). Plaintiff alleges that the county has a policy of settling all civil rights claims for a lump sum that includes both damages and fees. The alleged effect is to preclude any fee petitions and to cause many attorneys to refuse meritorious cases. The court issued a preliminary injunction forbidding the county to apply this policy to Bernhardt's case challenging the policy. As that formulation hints, it has been difficult to set up a test case for this issue.

A similar allegation of a fixed policy appears in Pony v. County of Los Angeles, 433 F.3d 1138 (9th Cir. 2006), *cert. denied,* 126 S.Ct. 2864 (2006). The County denies having such a policy; the court cites 20 years of intermittent litigation by the same attorney trying to raise the issue. The court holds that the right to fees belongs to the client, that that right is nonassignable, and that a contract purporting to assign the fee award or agree not to accept a settlement without fees is unenforceable. The court also holds that the attorney lacks standing to challenge the county's alleged policy of universal fee waivers, because the client, who holds the right to fees, does not want to assert that right, and because the lawyer cannot show injury in fact because the outcome of the litigation without a fee waiver is entirely speculative.

There is no reason in principle that a lump sum settlement could not be large enough to cover both damages and fees. But there is the *Rivera* problem; if the damages are small in proportion to the cost of litigation, a standard contingent fee agreement will undercompensate the lawyer. And it would be difficult to write, or negotiate, a contract in which the client agreed to divide the lump sum based on a lodestar calculation.

Page 953. After note 7, add:

7.1. The Ninth Circuit has rejected a class settlement in which plaintiff and defendant negotiated a fee based on the common fund theory. Staton v. Boeing Co., 327 F.3d 938 (9th Cir. 2003). Class counsel settled an employment discrimination claim for $6.5 million in cash to the class, plus injunctive relief that the court characterized as "largely precatory" but that counsel valued at $3.65 million, plus $4.05 million to class counsel as attorneys' fees. The parties characterized this as an award of 28% of the common fund consisting of the cash to the class, the cash to counsel, and the value of the injunctive relief.

The court said it is permissible to negotiate a lump sum that includes both merits relief and fees, and for counsel to then petition the court for a common fund fee award -- even in cases such as this one where plaintiffs could have sought a lodestar award under the fee-shifting provisions of the employment discrimination laws. But the majority held that plaintiff and defendant cannot negotiate the fee to be awarded out of a common fund; they can negotiate only the total amount, and class counsel must petition the court for any award based on the common fund theory. No one represented the class in this negotiation of common fund fees between class counsel and defendant. And defendant's need to know the bottom line, which justified simultaneous negotiation of fees and merits in *Jeff D.*, did not justify simultaneous negotiation here; defendant already knew the bottom line.

Page 956. After note 10, add:

The latest opinion in the case is White v. General Motors Corp., 835 So.2d 892 (La. Ct. App. 2002). The court prohibits, as inconsistent with the settlement agreement, further attempts by plaintiffs' counsel to create a working secondary market in the settlement certificates.

Page 956. After note 11, add:

The Vermont Supreme Court has held that the Alabama court lacked jurisdiction over 900 Vermont class members and that the judgment is not binding on them. The court found inadequate representation and inadequate notice; it characterized *Hoffman* as a defendant class action in which lawyers sought fees from class members who stood to incur liability rather than a remedy. State v. Homeside Lending, Inc., 826 A.2d 997 (Vt. 2003).

Presumably the Vermont court can order the defendant lenders to restore funds taken from the escrow accounts of Vermont borrowers. It is not clear that Vermont has any way to enable these lenders to recover these sums from class counsel; the lenders may actually have to pay out of their own pocket.

Page 958. After note 15, add:

16. Congress has attempted to address some of these problems in the Class Action Fairness Act of 2005, codified at 28 U.S.C. §§1332, 1453, and 1711 *et seq.* It creates federal jurisdiction over class actions with more than $5 million in controversy and one or more class members with citizenship diverse from one or more defendants. State class actions that satisfy these requirements may be removed to federal court on motion of any defendant, even if one or more defendants resides in the state where the action is pending. There are exceptions for class actions substantially centered in a single state, and the act does not apply to cases filed before its

enactment. Once in federal court, related class actions may be transferred for pretrial purposes to a single district judge. 28 U.S.C. §1407 (2000). From the perspective of class members, the act has the potential to eliminate reverse auctions in cases where it applies, but at the expense of moving these cases from state courts to federal courts that, given the current political alignment, are often less friendly.

Other sections of the act provide that contingent fees in coupon settlements shall be based on the coupons actually redeemed, not on the coupons distributed; that in class actions against financial institutions, state or federal bank supervisors shall be notified of any proposed settlement; and that proposed settlements resulting in a net loss to any class member may be approved "only if the court makes a written finding that nonmonetary benefits to the class member substantially outweigh monetary loss."

17. The *Jeff D.* litigation, filed in 1980 and originally settled in 1983, continues on. There is a good account in Jonathan Martin, *A Force for Change*, Spokane Spokesman-Review (Oct. 6, 2002), available at *www.childrensalliance.org/4Download/lostchildren4.pdf*, and a summary review in a recent opinion reporting findings of fact from a two-week contempt hearing. Jeff D. v. Kempthorne, 2007 WL 461471 (D. Idaho, Feb. 7, 2007). The case has been settled repeatedly with three consent decrees and additional subsidiary agreements along the way, but the state never provided the money to implement the consent decrees and it sought and received repeated extensions of deadlines. In 2000, an angry judge credibly threatened contempt sanctions, and for a time, the pace of progress seemed to improve. The parties negotiated an Implementation Plan with 50 Recommendations and with Action Items under each Recommendation. *Id.* at *2.

Apparently in the midst of this negotiation, the state moved to vacate the entire decree unless plaintiffs proved that it was still needed to end a constitutional violation. Not only would this require plaintiffs to prove their case all over again, but recall the state's earlier position that it had given the children more than the Constitution required in exchange for the waiver of attorneys' fees. Assuming that accurately characterized the bargain, the state now proposed to keep the fee waiver while insisting that the children could not have anything more than the constitutional minimum. In the wake of Frew v. Hawkins, described in the supplement to pages 342 and 492, the court of appeals had no trouble rejecting the state's motion to modify or vacate the decree. Jeff D. v. Kempthorne, 365 F.3d 844 (9th Cir. 2004). In the court's words, "The history of this case is a sad record of promises made and broken over two decades." *Id.* at 847. The court has consistently held that the fee waiver does not apply to fees incurred in post-waiver efforts to enforce the consent decree. *Id.* at 855; Jeff D. v. Andrus, 899 F.2d 753, 765 (9th Cir. 1989).

Emphasizing that an order must be "both specific and definite" to support a finding of contempt, 2207 WL 461471 at *3, and requiring clear and convincing evidence of a substantial failure to comply, not based on a "good faith and reasonable interpretation of the judgment," *id.* at *3, *53, the court found Idaho officials in contempt with respect to 21 Action Items. It found that plaintiffs had failed to carry their burden of proof with respect to many other charges of contempt. The court ordered defendants to substantially comply with the 21 Action Items within 120 days, and then said, "Once the defendants are in compliance with these Action Items, the defendants may file a motion to vacate the consent decrees pursuant to Federal Rule of Procedure 60(b)." *Id.* at *54. After 27 years of resistance and delay, can a brief period of substantial compliance possibly justify any confidence that defendants will continue to comply without continued judicial supervision?

B. UNCONSCIONABILITY AND THE EQUITABLE CONTRACT DEFENSES

Page 977. After note 7, add:

7.1. On remand in *Adams*, Circuit City's arbitration agreement was held unconscionable on the authority of *Armendariz*. 279 F.3d 889 (9th Cir. 2002). But the same panel upheld the agreement as applied to another employee. Circuit City Stores, Inc. v. Ahmed, 283 F.3d 1198 (9th Cir. 2002). The difference was that Ahmed was given a 30-day opportunity to opt out, and told that he could continue working at Circuit City even if he opted out. Because he had a genuine option, the agreement was not procedurally unconscionable. The opinion does not indicate how many employees were given this option; more important, it does not indicate what percentage opted out of an agreement already held to be substantively unconscionable.

7.2. The law firm O'Melveny & Myers tried to impose an arbitration agreement on its employees, but the agreement was held unconscionable. Davis v. O'Melveny & Myers, 485 F.3d 1066 (9th Cir. 2007). The agreement was procedurally unconscionable because incumbent employees had to accept the agreement or resign; with no real choice, it was irrelevant that they got 90 days to think about it. And the court found four clauses substantively unconscionable. A short limitations provisions made no allowance for undiscovered or continuing violations. A confidentiality clause was so stringent it precluded reasonable efforts to investigate the claim, and it bound only employees, not the firm. The arbitration agreement itself did not bind the firm. And the agreement barred employees from filing claims with regulatory agencies that depended "on an employee's willingness to come forward, in support of the public good." *Id.* at 1083. Plaintiff was a paralegal who sued under the Fair Labor Standards Act and California labor regulation, alleged that she had not been paid for overtime and had been denied lunch breaks and rest breaks. The arbitration agreement purported to bind all "employees," explicitly including associates, but apparently not partners.

7.3. The Supreme Court has reaffirmed an important limitation on the right to challenge arbitration clauses. *Buckeye Check Cashing, Inc. v. Cardegna*, 546 U.S. 440 (2006). *Buckeye* involved a claim that a contract was illegal rather than unconscionable, but I can think of no reason why its rule should not apply to either kind of claim. If a litigant claims that the arbitration clause itself is illegal, that claim can be decided in court. But if he claims that the whole contract is illegal, on grounds not specific to the arbitration clause, that claim is to be decided by the arbitrator. The alleged source of illegality in *Buckeye* was usury and related violations of consumer lending statutes, and those issues went to the arbitrator. Similarly, the courts could decide Armendariz's claim that the arbitration clause was unconscionable, but if he claimed that the contract was unconscionable on some other ground, that issue would presumably be for the arbitrator.

Page 978. After note 9, add:

9.1. Little v. Auto Stiegler, Inc., 63 P.3d 979 (Cal. 2003), holds unconscionable a clause providing that only arbitration awards in excess of $50,000 could be appealed. At least in the employment context, this meant that the employer could appeal serious losses, and the employee could not -- save in the very rare case where the employee might be the defendant.

But in contrast to *Armendariz*, the Court said this clause was separable from the rest of the arbitration agreement. A single unconscionable clause did not permeate the agreement, and the clause could be deleted without requiring a judge-made substitute to restore a workable agreement.

In re Halliburton Co., 80 S.W.3d 566 (Tex. 2002), upholds an arbitration agreement that may be a model of how to impose an arbitration agreement that will not be unconscionable. The agreement provided for discovery under the federal rules and for any remedy available in court, and for attorneys' fees to a successful employee whether or not fees would be available in court. The employer paid all expenses of arbitration, and up to $2,500 for the employee to consult with an attorney; the employee paid a $50 filing fee. The principal benefit to the employer would seem to be avoidance of jury trial.

The Fourth Circuit, commonly described as the most conservative in the country, has held several arbitration agreements unconscionably one-sided. The cases are collected in Murray v. United Food & Commercial Workers, 289 F.3d 297, 301-305 (4th Cir. 2002).

D. LACHES AND LIMITATIONS

2. Statutes of Limitations

Page 1009. After note 4, add:

4.1. The Supreme Court has sharply limited *Bazemore*. Ledbetter v. Goodyear Tire & Rubber Co., 127 S.Ct. 2162 (2007). In plaintiff's job category, Goodyear conducted annual performance reviews and then set salaries on the basis of merit. Plaintiff proved, to the satisfaction of a jury, that this process had long discriminated on the basis of sex, with the result that her pay was now far lower than that of men with similar experience and doing the same work. But she did not prove any discrimination in the most recent pay raises. The Court held, in an opinion by Justice Alito, that each "pay setting decision" was a "discrete act," and if discriminatory, a discrete violation. *Id.* at 2165. Subsequent unequal paychecks were not new discriminatory acts, but merely the present consequence of past discriminatory acts.

The Court distinguished *Bazemore* as a case where the employer maintained "a discriminatory pay structure." *Id.* at 2173. *Bazemore* did not apply "when an employer issues paychecks pursuant to a system that is 'facially nondiscriminatory and neutrally applied,'" *id.* at 2174, quoting Lorance v. AT&T Technologies, Inc., 490 U.S. 900, 911 (1989). *Lorance* was a seniority case, overruled with respect to seniority by the Civil Rights Act of 1991. The pay system in *Bazemore* gave equal raises every year on a discriminatory base, but any complaint about that discriminatory base was long since

160

barred. It is not clear why the *Bazemore* employer's system of equal annual raises was not "nondiscriminatory and neutrally applied," even though applied to a discriminatory base now insulated from judicial attack. Maybe the Court's distinction is that in *Bazemore*, all black employees hired before 1972 had lower pay than their white peers; maybe it is the number of victims that makes a pay "structure" discriminatory. Or maybe it was the openness of the past discrimination in *Bazemore*. We can only draw inferences; the distinction is wholly unexplained.

Plaintiff in *Ledbetter* particularly emphasized a past supervisor who had given discriminatory performance reviews; the statute of limitations had run on those reviews. But suppose she had cast her complaint and evidence purely in the present. Suppose she had simply said: "I am the only woman in my supervisory job category. I make $3700 a month; the 15 men make from $4200 to $5200 a month. This disparity cannot be based on job performance; I got a 'Top Performance Award' just two years ago. There is no explanation for this pay disparity except sex discrimination." This is not a hypothetical; the specific facts in that argument are true. Would that claim be barred by limitations? Would it be a substantive defense for Goodyear to explain that it had discriminated against Ledbetter years ago (or at least, more than six months ago), and that her pay in earlier years was a neutral fact that explained her unequal pay today? The Court does say that "a freestanding violation may always be charged within its own charging period regardless of its connection to other violations." *Id.*

Justice Ginsburg dissented for four. She feared that the Court has insulated systemic pay discrimination. Suppose that each year, the men get a slightly larger raise than Ledbetter. In year 1, the pay difference would be small, and the reasons for the difference might be unclear. If Ledbetter does not sue, that decision becomes insulated from judicial review; if she sues and loses, the finding of no discrimination in year 1 becomes binding. Either way, the events of year 1 are legally insulated when she sues over a similar small disparity in year 2. There might never be a time when she can successfully sue. Could the pattern of disparate raises over the years be evidence of discriminatory intent in year x, even though she cannot sue over the earlier years? The Court does not say.

Page 1011. After note 9, add:

Predictions are dangerous things. *Morgan* was reversed only in part. National Railroad Passenger Corp. v. Morgan, 536 U.S. 101 (2002). With respect to "discrete" discriminatory acts, the Court unanimously applied the separate accrual rule. The claim for each discriminatory act was barred 300 days after it occurred.

But, the Court said, "Hostile environment claims are different in kind from discrete acts. . . . A hostile work environment claim is comprised of a series of separate acts that collectively constitute one 'unlawful employment practice'" (internal quotation from the statute). As long as the hostile acts that created the hostile environment are sufficiently related, plaintiff may recover for the entire hostile environment, including the part that happened more than 300 days before plaintiff filed. But such claims may be barred by laches if plaintiff delays unreasonably and defendant is prejudiced. Justice Thomas wrote the opinion, with Justices Stevens, Souter, Ginsburg, and Breyer making up his majority. The remaining four conservatives dissented, arguing that the acts creating the hostile environment should also be divided into those that occurred within and without the 300-day limit.

The opinion partly turns on certain anomalies in the federal employment discrimination laws. Although the statute has a 300-day statute of limitations (and once had a 180-day statute), it also provides that no back pay may be recovered for any period more than two years prior to the filing of a charge. This would be anomalous if the separate accrual rule barred back pay for any period more than 300 days prior to the filing of a charge. The Court unanimously embraced that anomaly with respect to "discrete" violations, but a majority rejected it with respect to hostile environment claims.

The curious history of the two-year back-pay provision is set out in Douglas Laycock, *Continuing Violations, Disparate Impact in Compensation, and Other Title VII Issues*, 49 L. & Contemp. Probs. 53, 57 (No. 4, Autumn 1986). In the 1960s, the courts of appeals created a theory of liability for continuing effects of past discrimination. The principal example was the application of seniority systems to employees who had suffered past discrimination in promotion or job assignment, and thus should have been more senior. The continuing effects theory could impose liability for discrimination well outside the limitations period. Congress responded in the 1972 amendments with the two-year limit on back pay, which was then the only compensatory remedy available. In 1977, the Supreme Court rejected the continuing effects theory, leaving few situations to which the two-year limit on back pay could apply. Prior to *Morgan*, the most plausible theory would have been that it places an outside limit on claims of the discovery rule, fraudulent concealment, and continuing violations. But the Court has never held that the discovery rule and fraudulent concealment are even available in Title VII claims, and the continuing violation theory is sharply limited in *Ledbetter*, discussed in this supplement to page 1009. Under *Morgan*, the two-year limit on back pay applies to hostile environment claims. In 1991, Congress authorized compensatory damages, including emotional distress, and the two-year limit on back pay does not apply to these damages. So the effect of *Morgan* appears to be that plaintiff can recover two years of back pay and five years of emotional distress.

Page 1011. After note 10, add:

11. Another example of plaintiff's option appears in Franconia Associates v. United States, 536 U.S. 129 (2002). The United States made low interest loans to persons who agreed to build low income housing, and to comply with restrictions designed to protect low income tenants for as long as the loan was outstanding. But, they alleged, under the original terms of the contract, they could prepay the loan at any time.

Congress became concerned that high rates of prepayment were reducing the low income housing stock, and in 1987, it amended the underlying statute to prohibit prepayments. At various later dates, plaintiffs tendered prepayment of their loans and the government refused to accept the payment. In 1997, plaintiffs sued, alleging breach of contract and a taking of property. Congress has consented to suits for breach of contract and for takings, and enacted a six-year statute of limitations.

The government argued that the statute ran from 1987, when Congress definitively eliminated the right to prepay. Plaintiffs argued that the statute ran from the various dates on which the government refused to accept their tendered repayments. The Court unanimously agreed with plaintiffs. Turning to the common law of contracts, the Court held that the government's alleged duty under the contracts was to accept prepayment when tendered; there was no breach until such a payment was refused. Statements that a contracting party will breach in the future, when the time for performance arrives, are called anticipatory repudiations; such a repudiation is treated as a breach only if plaintiff chooses to so treat it. The 1987 legislation was such a repudiation -- merely a statement that the government would breach in the future if the occasion arose. Congress could have changed its mind and passed new legislation, just as any party repudiating a contract can change his mind. Plaintiffs who did nothing when the legislation was passed can sue at any time within six years after their tendered prepayment is refused.

Page 1012. After note 4, add:

What about a statute enacted before 1990 and amended after 1990? The Court unanimously held that the four-year federal statute of limitations applies to claims arising under amendments enacted after 1990, and that in close cases, the test is whether the claim could have been brought before December 1, 1990. Jones v. R.R. Donnelley & Sons Co., 541 U.S. 369 (2004).

Graham County Soil & Water Conservation District v. United States ex rel. Wilson, 545 U.S. 409 (2005), involved a claim arising under a 1986 amendment to the False Claims Act, 31 U.S.C. §3731 (2000), which lets bounty hunters sue to recover money obtained by fraud against the United States. The act contains its own limitations period, but the Court concluded that that limitations period applies to only claims to recover the government's money, and not to Wilson's claim that her employer retaliated against her for filing a claim under the act. The grounds for this distinction are too complex and idiosyncratic to be worth explaining here, although I thought the two dissenters had much the better of the argument. So here's a case where Congress provided a statute of limitations that could plausibly have been read to apply, and even so the Court directed the lower courts to seek out analogous statutes in every jurisdiction.

A statute of limitations applicable to "every action for money damages" applies only to suits in court, and not to administrative proceedings to recover the same money. BP America Production Co. v. Burton, 127 S.Ct. 638 (2006). At least that is true for the particular statute of limitations before the Court, which involved government claims for underpaid royalties on oil and gas produced from government lands. And the rule that statutes of limitations do not run against the sovereign except to the extent that the legislature expressly says so was doing some of the work. But the Court also relied heavily on the view that "action" means a suit in court, and does not include administrative proceedings unless appropriately modified, as in "administrative actions." So the implications appear to be general for cases where there are alternative judicial and administrative forums.

Page 1013. After note 5, add:

5. Wallace v. Kato, 127 S.Ct. 1091 (2007), explores several accrual and tolling issues. Plaintiff, then fifteen years old, was arrested without a warrant and without probable cause. After questioning that continued through much of the night, he confessed to a murder. He was convicted, but the state appellate court reversed, and on a second appeal, held the confession to be the fruits of the illegal arrest. In 2002, eight years after the illegal arrest, the state dropped all charges. Plaintiff then sued the arresting officers under §1983.

Following Owens v. Okure (described in note 2), the Court applied Illinois's two-year statute of limitations for personal injury cases. And it tolled the statute of limitations for the two-and-a-half years that plaintiff was a minor.

But it said that the determination of when the cause of action accrued depends on federal law, not state law. The claim accrued when the tort was complete and some damage had been suffered, and that was as soon as he was arrested, back in 1994. The statute of limitations does not begin to run until the false imprisonment ends, presumably because plaintiff cannot be expected to sue while falsely imprisoned. But this was not much help, because the Court invoked an old common law distinction: arrest or imprisonment without legal process is false imprisonment; malicious or unfounded arrest or imprisonment pursuant to legal process is malicious prosecution. This claim was analogous to false imprisonment, because the officers had no warrant or other legal process. But legal process issued, and thus the false imprisonment ended, as soon as the state took plaintiff's confession to a judge and had him arraigned; now he was imprisoned (falsely or otherwise) pursuant to legal process. So the statute of limitations began to run as soon as he was arraigned. But for his minority, he should have sued in 1994; tolling for his minority, he should have sued within two years after he turned 18, that is, before his birthday in 1999. And all this was true even if he was claiming as consequential damages the entire period he spent in jail and prison pending trial and appeal. Damages do not have to be complete or even reasonably predictable for a cause of action to accrue.

Heck v. Humphrey, 512 U.S. 477 (1994), described in the main volume at page 145, held that no plaintiff can recover damages in federal court for "harm caused by actions whose unlawfulness would render a conviction or sentence invalid," unless the conviction or sentence has been reversed or expunged. But that rule did not apply here, because at the time plaintiff's cause of action accrued, he had not been convicted or even indicted. So there was no conviction to be interfered with. Probably the federal court would have stayed his §1983 action pending the outcome of the state prosecution, but even so, the statute of limitations was running.

Justice Breyer would have tolled the statute until the conviction was set aside; he thought the majority's rule would force criminal defendants with search-and-seizure issues to file protective §1983 claims just in case. That may happen for well-represented defendants; more likely, most defendants will not file such claims and the majority's rule will result in most of the few claims that turn out to have merit being barred by limitations. The majority thought Breyer's rule was unworkable; the Court would not toll limitations for a possible conviction that might never happen.

Page 1022. After note 7, add:

7.1. In National Railroad Passenger Corp. v. Morgan, 536 U.S. 101 (2002), Justice O'Connor wrote separately to say that the very short statute of limitations for employment discrimination claims should be subject to the discovery rule. Chief Justice Rehnquist and Justice Breyer joined that part of her opinion. Justices Scalia and Kennedy, who joined other parts of her opinion, dissociated themselves from the part about the discovery rule.

Scalia did find a basis for extending a limitations period in Young v. United States, 535 U.S. 43 (2002). He wrote for a unanimous Court that "It is hornbook law that limitations periods are 'customarily subject to "equitable tolling,"' unless tolling would be 'inconsistent with the text of the relevant statute.'" His string cite included *Holmberg v. Armbrecht.*

In *Young,* the Court held that the government's tax claims were tolled during the pendency of the taxpayer's earlier bankruptcy, because the automatic stay in bankruptcy precluded the government from filing any claims or taking any steps to collect. Tolling when plaintiff was legally precluded from suing is a much easier case for a defense-oriented judge than tolling when plaintiff failed to discover his claim.

Page 1023. After note 10, add:

11. The Court had some useful advice on the confusing usage in this area:

> Courts, including this Court, it is true, have been less than meticulous in this regard; they have more than occasionally used the term "jurisdictional" to describe emphatic time prescriptions in rules of court. . . . Clarity would be facilitated if courts and litigants used the label "jurisdictional" not for claim-processing rules, but only for prescriptions delineating the classes of cases (subject matter jurisdiction) and the persons (personal jurisdiction) falling within the court's adjudicatory authority.

Kontrick v. Ryan, 540 U.S. 443, 454 (2004). The Court repeated the distinction between jurisdictional rules and claim-processing rules in Scarborough v. Principi, 541 U.S. 401 (2004), summarized at supplement to page 493. Justice Ginsburg wrote both opinions. In *Kontrick*, the Court said the proper question was "'whether the time restrictions . . . are in such "emphatic form"' as to preclude equitable exceptions." *Id.* at 458, quoting the amicus brief of the United States. The issue in *Kontrick* was an untimely objection to an untimely motion; the Court held that the objection was waived. The party with the untimely objection argued unsuccessfully that the *other* side's time limit was jurisdictional, so that the objection could be raised at any time.

Justice Ginsburg continued her campaign to stamp out the idea of jurisdictional time limits in Day v. McDonough, 547 U.S. 198 (2006), and Arbaugh v. Y & H Corp., 546 U.S. 500 (2006), although each case involved somewhat different issues. *Day* holds that a judge in a habeas corpus case can raise the statute of limitations sua sponte, without a motion from defendant, although, Justice Ginsburg carefully explained for the Court, this is *not* because the limitations period is jurisdictional. *Arbaugh* arose under the employment discrimination provisions of the Civil Rights Act of 1964, which apply only to employers with 15 or more employees. The Court held that the number of employees -- and, it strongly suggested, similar threshold questions concerning the applicability of other federal laws -- is a question on the merits, is not a question of jurisdiction, and is waived if not raised in timely fashion. Both opinions recite and reaffirm the holding in *Kontrick*. See also the per curiam in Eberhart v. United States, 546 U.S. 12 (2005), again explaining that time limits are not jurisdictional and applying *Kontrick* to a time limit in the Federal Rules of Criminal Procedure. That time limit says it cannot be extended, but the Court says its protections can be waived by not raising the issue in response to a late filing.

12. The Court has agreed to decide whether these decisions apply to suits against the United States. John R. Sand & Gravel Co. v. United States, 457 F.3d 1345 (Fed. Cir. 2006), *cert. granted*, 2007 WL 594691 (May 29, 2007). The Federal Circuit held these cases irrelevant, because limitation provisions in statutes consenting to suits against the United States are a condition on the waiver of

sovereign immunity, and therefore jurisdictional. The dissenter noted that the Supreme Court had rejected a similar argument, also based on sovereign immunity, for a stringent interpretation of when claims against the United States accrue. Franconia Associates v. United States, 536 U.S. 129, 145 (2003), described in this supplement to page 1011. The test of the statute also seems to distinguish limitations from jurisdiction: "Every claim of which the United States Court of Federal Claims has jurisdiction shall be barred unless the petition thereon is filed within six years after such claim first accrues." 28 U.S.C. §2501 (2000). *But see* Raygor v. Regents of University of Minnesota, 534 U.S. 533 (2002), described in this supplement to page 493, relying on sovereign immunity to preclude tolling the statute of limitations against a state.

Page 1024. After note 3, add:

4. Of course, defendants and courts may resist recharacterizing the claim. A good example is EC Term of Years Trust v. United States, 127 S.Ct. 1763 (2007), where the IRS seized property belonging to a trust to collect taxes owed by taxpayers who had created the trust. The trust sued for a tax refund under a section of the Internal Revenue Code that allows two years to file an administrative claim and two years after denial of that claim to file a refund suit. But another section of the Code specifically authorizes a suit for wrongful levy by any person other than the taxpayer who claims an interest in property seized, and that claim must be filed within nine months. Noting that "[i]n a variety of contexts, the Court has held that a precisely drawn, detailed statute pre-empts more general remedies," *id.* at 1767, quoting Brown v. General Services Administration, 425 U.S 820, 834 (1976), the Court held the wrongful-levy section to be the exclusive remedy and its shorter statute of limitations to be unavoidable.

Page 1031. After note 11, add:

As expected, *Chapman* was reversed. King Ranch, Inc. v. Chapman, 118 S.W.3d 742 (Tex. 2003). The court found no evidence of extrinsic fraud, which it defined very narrowly; fraud or conflict of interest on the part of Chapman's attorney did not count.

CHAPTER TEN

REMEDIES AND SEPARATION OF POWERS

A. IMPLIED RIGHTS OF ACTION

Page 1038. After note 4, add:

4.1. The Court has quit describing *Bivens* as a rule with limits and exceptions. Its most recent opinion describes *Bivens* actions as merely a possibility, requiring a fresh decision whether to create a remedy with respect to every alleged constitutional right:

> The first question is whether to devise a new *Bivens* damages action [for plaintiff's claim of government harassment and retaliation based on his refusal to give the government, without compensation, an easement across his ranch]. *Bivens* held that the victim of a Fourth Amendment violation by federal officers had a claim for damages, and in the years following we have recognized two more nonstatutory damages remedies, the first for employment discrimination in violation of the Due Process Clause, *Davis*, and the second for an Eighth Amendment violation by prison officials, *Carlson*. But we have also held that any freestanding damages remedy for a claimed constitutional violation has to represent a judgment about the best way to implement a constitutional guarantee; it is not an automatic entitlement no matter what other means there may be to vindicate a protected interest, and in most instances we have found a *Bivens* remedy unjustified. We have accordingly held against applying the *Bivens* model to claims of First Amendment violations by federal employers, *Bush*, harm to military personnel through activity incident to service, *Stanley*, and wrongful denials of Social Security disability benefits, *Schweiker*. We have seen no case for extending *Bivens* to claims against federal agencies, *Meyer*, or against private prisons, *Malesko*.

Wilkie v. Robbins, 2007 WL 1804315 (U.S., June 25, 2007). This was Justice Souter, writing for a majority of seven. This passage seems to reinstate the claim-by-claim approach that the Court appeared to reject in *Davis* and *Carlson*. And this paragraph seems to require plaintiff to show why a new remedy should be "devise[d]," although the next paragraph again speaks of "special factors counselling hesitation" and the existence of alternate remedies that amount "to a convincing reason for the Judicial Branch to refrain from creating a new and freestanding remedy in damages."

Justices Scalia and Thomas wrote separately to say that *Bivens* and its progeny were relics of another era and should be "limited 'to the precise circumstances that they involved,'" quoting *Malesko*, 534 U.S. at 75 (Scalia, J., concurring). Justices Ginsburg and Stevens dissented.

The case was odd. Robbins owned a guest ranch in Wyoming that consisted of one main parcel and some noncontiguous parcels, largely surrounded by federal land. Shortly before he bought the ranch, his seller had conveyed an easement to the United States, allowing public access to a scenic mountain area on the ranch. But the United States failed to record the easement, Robbins knew nothing about it, and he therefore took free of it. When the government demanded that he grant them a new easement, without any additional compensation, he refused. Government employees then began what Justice Ginsburg called "a seven-year campaign of relentless harassment and intimidation to force Robbins to give in," and what Justice Souter described as "enforc[ing] the law to the letter," sometimes overreaching, and occasional common law torts. Souter thought that Robbins had a remedy for each individual government action; Ginsburg disputed that. But both agreed that Robbins had no effective remedy for the pattern of government action.

But Souter saw a special factor counseling hesitation: there was no workable way to define Robbins's cause of action. His claim was rooted in the Takings Clause; the government wanted his property, and it did not want to pay compensation. But the government was entitled to engage in hard bargaining, and Souter saw no workable way to define when the government had gone too far.

Page 1048. After note 1, add:

1.1. The Court rejected the reliance on §1983 in Justice Stevens' *Alexander* dissent, and dealt §1983 a major blow, in Gonzaga University v. Doe, 536 U.S. 273 (2002). (Gonzaga is a private institution, but the state court held that it had acted under color of law when it released confidential student information to state officials. This debatable holding was not at issue in the Supreme Court. Just assume Gonzaga was public.)

Like *Alexander*, *Gonzaga* was a suit under a Spending Clause statute, the Family Educational Rights and Privacy Act of 1974, 20 U.S.C. §1232g (2000) (FERPA). But this time, plaintiff also pleaded a §1983 claim. The Court acknowledged that §1983 creates a private remedy, but it said that remedy applies only to private rights, and private rights cannot be implied; Congress must create them. "A court's role in discerning whether personal rights exist in the §1983 context should therefore not differ from its role in discerning whether personal rights exist in the implied right of action context." Finding no express rights-creating language, the Court held that FERPA creates no private rights and cannot be enforced in a §1983 suit.

If §1983 actions are available only where Congress separately creates a private cause of action, then §1983 is effectively repealed, or perhaps reduced to a provision for attorneys' fees. The Court plainly does not go that far. Individual constitutional rights have long been interpreted to expressly create private rights, although they are do not expressly create private rights of action. Few constitutional provisions would create private rights if interpreted under the Court's new interpretive rules ("Congress shall make no law . . ." focuses on what government can and cannot do, not mentioning the rights of any individual), but it is surely inconceivable for the Court to now hold that the Bill of Rights creates no private rights. And perhaps the Court will not undo private enforcement of statutes that have long been held to create private rights. But it is a reasonable prediction that the Court will not find any more (or at least not many more) such rights-creating statutes. FERPA itself repeatedly referred to "the rights" of students and their parents, but that was not enough. This opinion goes far toward reducing §1983 claims to enforce federal statutes to the same status as implied rights of action.

The Court's reasoning does not seem limited to Spending Clause statutes, but the opinion emphasized how rarely the Court had permitted §1983 suits to enforce such statutes. It is possible that statutes not tied to spending might fare better.

1.2. There is a less alarming interpretation of *Gonzaga* in Sabree v. Richman, 367 F.3d 180 (3d Cir. 2004). *Sabree* holds that Medicaid provisions of the Social Security Act, which say that a state accepting federal funds "must provide . . . medical assistance . . . to . . . all [eligible] individuals" (ellipses and brackets by the court), creates a private right. The court assumes that *Gonzaga* did not overrule earlier cases finding private rights to enforce various federal statutes.

1.3. In City of Rancho Palos Verdes v. Abrams, 544 U.S. 113 (2005), the Court summarized the availability of §1983 remedies for statutory violations as consisting of two rules. The statute violated must create "an individually enforceable right," *Gonzaga*, and it must not explicitly or implicitly show "that Congress did not intend" for the §1983 remedy to be available, *Sea Clammers*. The Court seems to say that plaintiff must show an individually enforceable right but that defendant must show that Congress did not intend the §1983 remedy.

In the case before it, the Court held that a provision of the Telecommunications Act of 1996, 47 U.S.C. §332(c)(7) (2000), which limits the power of local governments to exclude or regulate communications towers, implicitly precludes a §1983 remedy. It provides for expedited judicial review, and does not provide for attorneys' fees; a §1983 remedy would avoid the time limits and trigger a right to fees. The decision was unanimous as to the result.

1.4. There is a fight over the reach of *Alexander* in Global Crossing Telecommunications, Inc. v. Metrophones Telecommunications, Inc., 127 S.Ct. 1513 (2007). The statutory scheme is too complex to fully explain here, but the statute expressly authorizes suits for damages caused by any "unjust or unreasonable" practice, and it gives regulatory power to the Federal Communications Commission. The Court thought that was enough to justify damage suits for violating the FCC regs. Justice Scalia dissented. He would allow suits for violating "interpretative regulations," which interpreted what was "unjust or unreasonable" within the meaning of the statute, but not for "substantive regulations" that created new prohibitions not found in the statute. He thought there was nothing unjust or unreasonable about what defendant had done apart from the fact that the FCC prohibited it. A majority of seven, including Roberts and Alito, rejected the relevance of Scalia's distinction between interpretive and substantive regulations, at least in this context. But the Court's view in *Alexander* would seem to be that those regulations were "substantive" in these terms; the regs prohibited what the statute did not.

Page 1051. After note 8, add:

8.1. *Franklin* is further limited in Barnes v. Gorman, 536 U.S. 181 (2002). *Barnes* holds that even where a court may order "any appropriate relief" under *Franklin*, punitive damages are not appropriate relief for violating a civil rights statute that applies to programs receiving federal financial assistance. Where civil rights compliance is a condition on the receipt of federal funds, violating the condition is a breach of contract, and punitive damages are not an appropriate remedy for breach of contract.

8.2. The Court has held that there is an implied right of action for retaliation under Title IX. Jackson v. Birmingham Board of Education, 544 U.S. 167 (2005). Plaintiff was the girls' basketball coach; he complained that the school discriminated against the girls' team, and he was fired. Employment discrimination statutes commonly prohibit retaliation, but there is no retaliation provision in Title IX, which prohibits discrimination "on the basis of sex." The Title IX regulations prohibit retaliation, but *Alexander* precluded reliance on the regs.

Justice O'Connor for the majority held that "when a funding recipient retaliates against a person *because* he complains of sex discrimination, this constitutes intentional 'discrimination' 'on the basis of sex,'" in violation of the statutory text. *Id.* at 174. And although Spending Clause legislation requires clear notice of what is forbidden to those who accept the money, the Board should have been put on notice by earlier cases broadly interpreting Title IX and also Title VI, the statute at issue in *Alexander*. And besides that, Title IX would be unenforceable if schools were free to fire or expel anyone who complained of sex discrimination. Justice Thomas, dissenting for the four you would expect, thought it obvious that plaintiff's sex (male) had nothing to do with his discharge; the school had discriminated on the basis of making a complaint, not on the basis of sex. Justice Thomas said "the majority returns this Court to the days in which it created remedies out of whole cloth to effectuate its vision of congressional purpose," substituting "its policy judgment for the bargains struck by Congress, as reflected in the statute's text." *Id.* at 195.

C. GOVERNMENTAL IMMUNITIES

1. Suits Against the Government

Page 1076. After note 6.b., add:

The Pugaches are the subjects of a documentary movie, *Crazy Love*, which has triggered a new round of news coverage, including a long feature story in the Washington Post. Paul Schwartzman, *Love's Acid Test: She Spurned Him, He Maimed her, and They Lived Happily Ever After, Sort of*, Wash. Post., June 6, 2007, available at 2007 WLNR 10537289.

Page 1082. After the third paragraph of note 2, add:

A somewhat more generous approach is illustrated in United States v. White Mountain Apache Tribe, 537 U.S. 465 (2003), under the parallel Indian Tucker Act, 28 U.S.C. §1505 (2000). The United States held and managed property in trust for the tribe, and allowed that property to deteriorate until $14 million was required to restore the buildings. The Court held that an express statutory provision that the government held the property in trust, together with the government's active management of the property, supported "a fair inference" that the government was liable as a trustee, apparently under principles analogous to the judge-made law of trusts. If an express cause of action were required, the law of trusts would be doing no work and the statutory declaration of trust would be irrelevant. The Court explained *Testan* as arising in a context where "the legal current is otherwise against the existence of a cognizable claim;" in such a context, "a fair inference will require an express provision." 537 U.S. at 478. It may not be too much to say that *White Mountain* recognizes an implied right of action.

The Court reached the opposite result in a companion case, United States v. Navajo Nation, 537 U.S. 488 (2003), finding that the United States had neither had nor exercised a trustee's responsibility for negotiating royalties on Indian coal mines, and thus had no liability for inadequate payments. The swing votes who distinguished the two cases were Justices O'Connor, Kennedy, and Breyer.

Page 1082. After note 3, add:

3.1. Orff v. United States, 545 U.S. 596 (2005), nicely illustrates the sort of trap that can lie hidden in immunity law. A sprawling, multi-party, multi-claim litigation about water rights in California's Central Valley mostly settled, leaving only one claim: farmers claiming to be third-party beneficiaries of a contract promising specified amounts of water to local water districts were suing the United States and federal officials for breach of that contract. The Reclamation Reform Act of 1982 gives consent "to join the United States as a necessary party defendant in any suit to adjudicate . . . the contractual rights of a contracting entity and the United States regarding any contract executed pursuant to a Federal reclamation law." 43 U.S.C. §390uu (2000). The Court unanimously held that the reference to "necessary party" meant that the United States could be joined only when its presence was necessary to complete adjudication of a dispute between other parties. That had been true when the litigation began, but when the case reduced to a simple contract claim against the United States, it was no longer within the scope of this waiver of immunity.

Of course the contract claim against the United States was within the Tucker Act, but the amount in controversy was more than

$10,000, so exclusive jurisdiction lay in the Court of Federal Claims. The claim could have been transferred there after the other parties dropped out. Your editor has not figured out whether it could still be transferred there, or refiled there, after a loss in the Supreme Court.

Page 1083. After note 4, add:

4.1. The United States may be liable for negligent safety inspections conducted in a state where a private safety inspector would be liable for similar negligence. United States v. Olson, 546 U.S. 43 (2005). Two miners were permanently disabled when a nine-ton slab of earth fell from the ceiling of the mine where they were working. The government had failed to inspect the site despite multiple grounds for finding a nondiscretionary duty to do so; the government abandoned its discretionary function argument in the Supreme Court. The Ninth Circuit had held that there is no private-sector equivalent to mine inspections, but that state and local agencies failing to inspect when required would be liable under the law of Arizona, where the case arose. The Supreme Court rejected both steps in that reasoning. The Tort Claims Act makes the United States liable where a "private person" would be liable, not where a state or local government would be liable. But the "circumstances" under which a private person would be liable need only be similar, not identical. So private safety inspectors provided a relevant analogy; they need not be mine inspectors. *Olson* and the cases on which it relies in effect hold that there is no public duty doctrine in the Tort Claims Act. In a state where private safety inspectors have liability and government safety inspectors do not (North Carolina is probably an example), the United States would be liable for negligent inspection by analogy to the private inspectors.

4.2. A claim arises in a foreign country if the wrongful conduct occurs there, even if the wrongful conduct was planned and directed from the United States. Sosa v. Alvarez-Machain, 542 U.S. 692 (2004). The Court feared that a "headquarters exception" would swallow the rule.

4.3. The actual wording of the postal exception is that the United States is not liable for "any claim arising out of the loss, miscarriage, or negligent transmission of letters or postal matters." 28 U.S.C.

§2680(b) (2000). The Supreme Court held that this language does not exclude liability for personal injuries allegedly suffered when plaintiff tripped over mail that a letter carrier negligently placed on her porch instead of in the mailbox. Dolan v. United States Postal Service, 546 U.S. 481 (2006). The Postal Service argued that leaving the mail for the recipient is the final step in "transmission," and thus that plaintiff had alleged "negligent transmission." The Court noted that on this theory, negligently driving a mail truck would also be negligent transmission of the mails, and that this would defeat a central purpose of the Tort Claims Act. It held that the meaning of "transmission" is limited by its association in the same phrase with "loss" and "miscarriage"; the clear intention of the exception is to exclude claims for lost or damaged mail. Justice Thomas filed a solitary and (in my view) unconvincing dissent.

4.4. The Court has agreed to review a somewhat similar issue in Ali v. Board of Prisons, 204 Fed. Appx. 778 (11th Cir. 2006), *cert. granted*, 2007 WL 278844 (May 29, 2007). The Tort Claims Act has an exception for "[a]ny claim arising in respect of the assessment or collection of any tax or customs duty, or the detention of any goods, merchandise, or other property by any officer of customs or excise or any other law enforcement officer." 28 U.S.C. 2680(c) (2000). There is a circuit split over whether "any other law enforcement officer" should be read as a freestanding addition to the rest of the exception, or whether it is limited by context to officers like customs officials and tax collectors, or to other officers assisting in the collection of customs or taxes. Prison officials -- pretty clearly law enforcement officers, but clearly not like customs or tax officials -- lost Ali's personal property, including legal papers and religious items, in the course of transferring him from one prison to another. Apart from whether prison officials are within the exception, is there a "detention" of property here? They didn't assess or collect a tax, and they didn't keep plaintiff's property; they just lost it. That question has not been argued or presented, and while it is clearly related to the question of what officers are covered, the Court might resist the conclusion that it is fairly included in the question on which cert was granted.

4.5. *The Westfall Act.* If a plaintiff sues a federal employee under state law, the Attorney General may certify that the employee was acting in the course and scope of his federal employment. The result of such a certification is that the case is removed to federal court, the claim against the employee is dismissed, the United States is substituted as the defendant, and the case proceeds under the Federal Tort Claims Act. This provision appears in the Federal Employee Liability Reform and Tort Compensation Act of 1988, 28 U.S.C. §2679(b) to (d) (2000), more commonly known as the Westfall Act for the case to which it responded, *Westfall v. Erwin*, 484 U.S. 292 (1988). *Westfall* held that federal employees are immune from state tort suits only for their discretionary acts, not for administrative acts. The Act makes federal employees absolutely immune for acts within the course and scope of their employment; the United States as the substituted defendant has the benefit of all the exceptions to the Tort Claims Act, including the discretionary function exception, but it absorbs the liability for torts not within any exception.

The Westfall Act has generated surprising complexities. The Attorney General may be tempted to protect federal employees by certifying freely, or he may be deterred by the prospect of the liability falling on the United States. Those conflicting incentives disappear when the United States is immune but the employee would not be. In Gutierrez de Martinez v. Lamagno, 515 U.S. 417 (1995), the Attorney General certified that a federal employee in Columbia, driving drunk with an unidentified woman after midnight, was acting within the scope of his employment. Maybe so. The Act says that the Attorney General's certification "shall conclusively establish scope of office or employment for purposes of removal." 28 U.S.C. §2679(d)(1)(2000). But the Court held that this certification is judicially reviewable for purposes of substituting defendants. If the court finds that the employee's action was not within the course and scope of his employment, the case can proceed against the employee.

4.6. In Osborn v. Haley, 127 S.Ct. 881 (2007), the Attorney General certified that the federal-employee defendant "was acting within the scope of his employment . . . at the time of the conduct alleged in the complaint. *Id.* at 889 n.2. But following removal to federal court, the United States denied that the "conduct alleged in the complaint" had ever happened. The Court held that this inconsistency -- nothing happened, but what did happen was in the course and scope of federal employment -- did not bar removal or substitution. It would make no sense if the Act protected guilty federal employees but failed to protect innocent federal employees. Justice Breyer dissented in part on this issue.

The district court had ruled the other way and remanded the case to state court. The Court held that this remand effectively denied the federal employee's immunity, and thus was an immediately appealable collateral order. See note 12 at 505 of the main volume. More dramatically, the Court held that the statutory provision making the Attorney General's certification binding for purposes of removal overrode 28 U.S.C. §1447(d), which precludes appellate review of district court orders remanding removed cases to the state courts. Justices Scalia and Thomas dissented on this issue.

Page 1084. After note 1, add:

1.1. The Court unanimously refused to create exceptions to this rule in Northern Insurance Co. v. Chatham County, 547 U.S. 189 (2006). Chatham County's negligent operation of a drawbridge inflicted $130,000 in damage on plaintiff's insured. The county argued that it should have some sort of ill-defined "residual immunity," not derived from the Eleventh Amendment, and perhaps special to admiralty cases or to cases where a local government performed essential state functions in admiralty. This claim to an exception would probably not have been cert worthy, except that it prevailed in the court of appeals under a circuit precedent from 1952. The Court unanimously held that sovereign immunity is based on the states' sovereign status prior to ratification of the Constitution. On that criterion, states were sovereign and counties were not, and it would not consider special rules for specific kinds of claims.

2. Suits Against Officers -- Absolute Immunity

Page 1101. After note 11, add:

11.1. If the legislature as a body intervenes in a lawsuit to defend the constitutionality of a statute that the Attorney General refused to defend, the Third Circuit has held that the legislature forfeits its immunity and becomes liable for attorneys' fees that would otherwise have been awarded against the executive. Planned Parenthood v. Attorney General, 297 F.3d 253 (3d Cir. 2002). The court reasoned that the legislature was acting as the executive and should be treated as the executive.

D. THE RIGHT TO JURY TRIAL

Page 1117. After note 2, add:

2.1. John Langbein at Yale has persuasively rejected this whole line of ERISA cases. John H. Langbein, *What ERISA Means by "Equitable": The Supreme Court's Trail of Error in Russell, Mertens, and Great-West*, 103 Colum. L. Rev. 1317 (2003). A pension or benefits plan is a trust for the benefit of the employees, and ERISA was consciously modeled on trust law. Equity courts had exclusive jurisdiction over trusts, and awarded make-whole relief in trust cases, so in a trust context, even consequential damages are appropriate equitable relief. The Court's error has been to ignore the trust context, and to try to distinguish legal from equitable remedies as if the question had arisen in a context where equitable jurisdiction depended on the remedy to be awarded, instead of depending on the substance of the underlying dispute. This is the body of law on which Justice Kennedy unsuccessfully relied in *Terry*, but which the Court rejected in *Mertens*. Langbein also notes that *Great-West* is probably wrong even on the Court's, terms, because subrogation was an equitable remedy.

2.2. The Court addressed another variation in Sereboff v. Mid Atlantic Medical Services, Inc., 126 S.Ct. 1869 (2006). *Sereboff* was like *Great-West*, but with a difference the Court found dispositive. As in *Great-West*, the medical insurer sued the insured to recover medical expenses paid by the insurer. But in *Sereboff*, the insured had possession of the funds collected from the tortfeasor. And the insurer took the precaution of seeking a preliminary injunction requiring the insured to segregate enough of the funds collected from the tortfeasor to satisfy the insurer's claims. Before the trial court ruled on the preliminary injunction, the insured agreed to segregate the funds. So the insurer sought to recover a specific fund. In the

Supreme Court's view, the insurance contract created an equitable lien on any funds the insured received from the tortfeasor, and enforcing that equitable lien is appropriate equitable relief. And this time, it was unanimous.

2.3. The Court has agreed to hear another of these cases. LaRue v. DeWolff, Boberg & Associates, 450 F.3d 570 (4th Cir. 2006), *cert. granted*, 2007 WL 1730445 (June 18, 2007). One question presented is whether the historic equitable jurisdiction over trusts makes compensatory relief equitable when the defendant is a fiduciary for plaintiff -- in this case, the plan administrator who administered plaintiff's 401(k) retirement account. The second question presented is whether another section of ERISA creates a cause of action for individuals, which might avoid the whole problem and end the necessity to characterize all ERISA remedies as equitable.